MAKE YOUR OWN
JEWELRY

using metal, wire, paper and clay

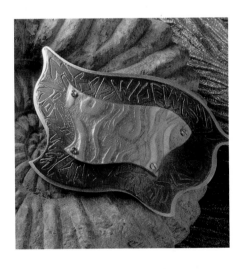

MAKE YOUR OWN
JEWELRY

using metal, wire, paper and clay

40 inspiring step-by-step projects for creating all kinds of stylish bangles,

brooches, earrings, rings, necklaces, hair accessories and trinket boxes

Edited by Ann Kay

southwater

This edition is published by Southwater

Southwater is an imprint of Anness Publishing Ltd
Hermes House, 88–89 Blackfriars Road, London SE1 8HA
tel. 020 7401 2077; fax 020 7633 9499
www.southwaterbooks.com; www.annesspublishing.com

If you like the images in this book and would like to investigate
using them for publishing, promotions or advertising, please visit
our website www.practicalpictures.com for more information.

© Anness Publishing Ltd 2006

UK agent: The Manning Partnership Ltd, 6 The Old Dairy,
Melcombe Road, Bath BA2 3LR; tel. 01225 478444;
fax 01225 478440; sales@manning-partnership.co.uk

UK distributor: Grantham Book Services Ltd, Isaac Newton Way,
Alma Park Industrial Estate, Grantham, Lincs NG31 9SD;
tel. 01476 541080; fax 01476 541061; orders@gbs.tbs-ltd.co.uk

North American agent/distributor: National Book Network,
4501 Forbes Boulevard, Suite 200, Lanham, MD 20706;
tel. 301 459 3366; fax 301 429 5746; www.nbnbooks.com

Australian agent/distributor: Pan Macmillan Australia,
Level 18, St Martins Tower, 31 Market St, Sydney, NSW 2000;
tel. 1300 135 113; fax 1300 135 103;
customer.service@macmillan.com.au

New Zealand agent/distributor: David Bateman Ltd,
30 Tarndale Grove, Off Bush Road, Albany, Auckland;
tel. (09) 415 7664; fax (09) 415 8892

A CIP catalogue record for this book is available from the
British Library.

Publisher: Joanna Lorenz
Editorial Director: Helen Sudell
Project Editor: Ann Kay
Copy-editor: Beverley Jollands
Designers: Design Principals, Nigel Partridge
Editorial Reader: Rosanna Fairhead
Production Controller: Pedro Nelson

Previously published as part of a larger volume, *Make Your Own Jewelry*

10 9 8 7 6 5 4 3 2 1

The publishers have made every effort to ensure that all instructions
contained within this book are accurate but cannot accept liability for
any resulting injury, damage or loss to persons or property, however it
may arise. Readers are reminded that due care and suitable
precautions (such as wearing goggles or gloves, for example) must be
taken when undertaking certain craft projects. Seek expert advice
about this if in any doubt.

Contents

Introduction

Everyone loves jewellery, whether to wear or to give, and it seems to fill a basic human need. Many of the oldest artefacts found by archaeologists have been personal ornaments, and all over the world jewellery has always been just as significant for its meaning as for its intrinsic beauty and worth. It's a universal symbol of wealth, power, love and desire. Yet the word "jewel" is derived from a Latin word for a plaything, and jewellery can certainly also be a source of pleasure and amusement. While you might keep family heirlooms such as pearls and diamonds in the bank, the pieces you choose to wear every day have a different kind of value – they're a daily delight and a perfect way to express your personality, especially if you've made them yourself.

This book takes a sideways look at the art of making jewellery in a range of inspiring ways, using approaches that require few specialist skills or costly raw materials. While it does include some beautiful, delicate pieces in silver and enamel, there are also surprising and original ideas for turning mundane ingredients such as clay and paper into characterful jewellery, transformed by clever paint and gilding techniques.

Beautiful photographs of around 40 lovely pieces are guaranteed to inspire you, whether you choose to follow the detailed step-by-step instructions to reproduce the designs exactly or use the techniques described as a springboard from which you can develop your own variations. The projects range

from simple brooches and necklaces that total beginners could manage without any difficulty to sophisticated etching and enamelling techniques: just follow the pliers symbols and tackle the simplest examples of each technique first. As well as the jewellery itself – from earrings, rings, pendants

and necklaces to bangles, hair decorations, buttons, pocket clips and cufflinks – you will also find a selection of beautiful boxes. Any of these would make an attractive addition to your dressing table, or would provide a wonderful way to present a handmade piece of jewellery as a gift.

Jewellery Fittings

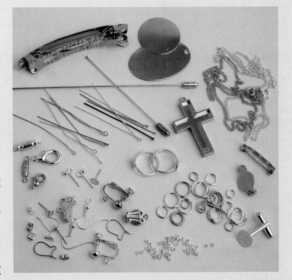

To make your own jewellery, you need a variety of fittings, such as necklace clasps, brooch pins, chains, metal pendant "blanks" that you can infill with enamel, and earring wires. The term "findings" is the name given to the many different parts used to fasten or link jewellery. The best-known findings include jump rings (the small metal rings used in all kinds of ways to link different parts of jewellery items – for example, to join the end of a string of beads to a clasp) and butterfly backs (for holding studs in place in pierced ears).

If you become very adept at metalwork, you might choose to make most of these kinds of things yourself, but in the meantime certain craft stores, and some jewellery stores, sell an enormous range of fittings to make jewellery-making really easy. You can also obtain fittings from the many companies selling them to the trade; most of these operate mail order schemes and have easily accessible websites.

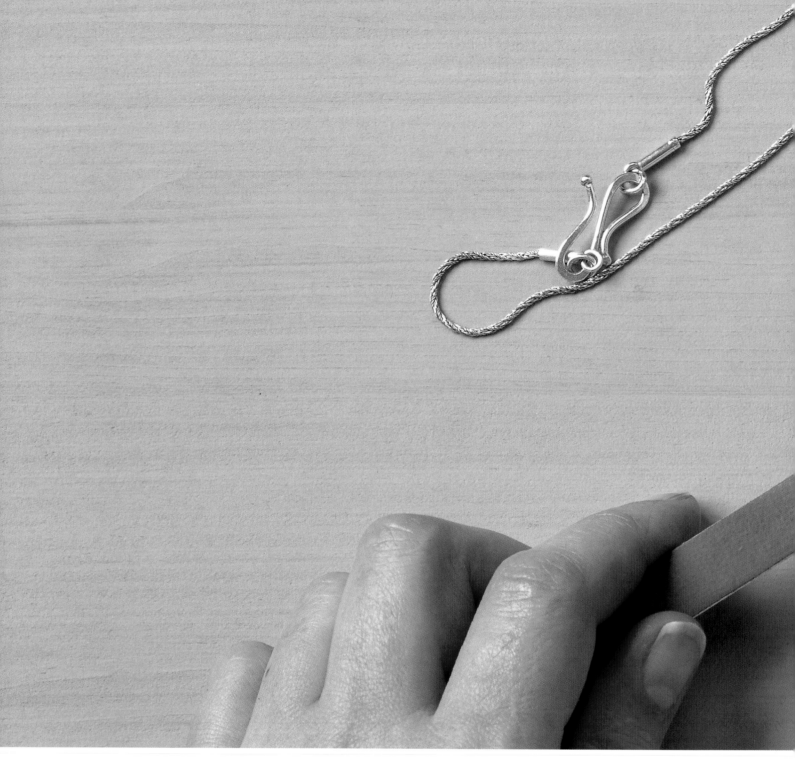

Enamelling and Metalwork

As soon as early people learnt how to work metal, they valued it as much for its beauty as its practical uses: the creation of jewellery, from delicate silver filigree to magical iron rings, has been an important skill in every civilization. Enamelling also has a long history of decorative use and early craftspeople used it in jewellery to imitate precious stones. Learning to use these materials in new designs continues a beautiful art and an ancient tradition.

Enamel is a form of glass and enamelling is the process of fusing it to metal using heat. Most materials need to be obtained from a specialist supplier: start by buying what you need for the simplest projects.

Enamelling Materials

Acids and pickles

Dilute solutions of various acids are used to degrease and de-oxidize metal before or after firing.

Ceramic fibre

This can be moulded to support awkwardly shaped pieces during firing.

Enamels

Jewellery enamels are available in lump or powder form, with or without lead. Leaded and lead-free enamels cannot be used together. Use transparent, translucent or opaque enamels to create different effects.

Enamel gum solution

Various organic gum solutions are available, some as sprays. Dilute solution is used to position cloisonné wires; a weak solution is used to hold powder enamel before firing. Use sparingly.

Etchants

Solutions of nitric and other acids are painted on metal to produce etched designs for filling with enamel.

Foil

Fine gold (23.5 ct) and silver (.995 ct) foil are available in a variety of thicknesses. Gold leaf is usually too thin for enamelling purposes.

Kaolin (ballclay, batwash)

This helps prevent enamel adhering to the firing support or the kiln floor.

Mica

In the technique called *plique-à-jour*, "windows" of translucent enamel are created in a pierced metal form. A sheet of mica can be used to support the enamel when firing such items.

Pumice powder

A pumice and water paste is used to polish enamel and metal after firing.

Resists

Stopping-out varnish can be painted on to areas of metal to be protected during etching. PnP blue acetate film produces a photographic resist.

Sheet metal

Copper and silver sheets come in various thicknesses and sections. Silver should be at least .925 (Sterling) quality. Avoid beryllium-containing copper.

Solder

Hard (4N, "IT" grade) silver solder should be used prior to enamelling.

Washing (baking) soda crystals

Use a soda solution to neutralize acids.

Water

In hard-water areas use bottled water or rainwater, as limescale and additives can impair the clarity of enamels.

Wire

Copper, fine silver and fine gold wire are available in rectangular section, pre-annealed, for cloisonné.

The main piece of equipment needed for enamelling is a domestic-sized gas or electric kiln. This and other specialist items are available from enamellers' and jewellers' suppliers.

Enamelling Equipment

Artist's brushes
Pure sable paintbrushes are the traditional tools for applying wet enamel.

Brass brush
Use a suede or other brass brush to clean metal after pickling.

Diamond-impregnated paper
This is a cleaner and faster abrasive than carborundum, the traditional abrasive for enamel, and is invaluable for concave surfaces.

Doming block, swage block, mandrel and punches
These blocks of steel, brass or hardwood are used to shape metal. Use a hammer with steel and brass blocks and a mallet with wood.

Felt polishing mop
Impregnated with pumice powder and water, a felt mop is used to polish fired enamel, either by hand or connected to an electric polishing motor.

Files
Use hand files to remove burrs after cutting metal. Diamond files can be used with water to abrade fired enamel.

Glass fibre brush
This will not scratch metal and can be used to clean enamel. Avoid contact with the hands.

Kiln
Electric kilns take longer to heat up to firing temperature than gas-fired kilns but are comparatively inexpensive. A regulator (thermostat) is needed to prevent overheating and a pyrometer gives an accurate temperature reading. Use ready-made firing supports or make them from stainless-steel mesh.

Pestle and mortar
Use only vitrified porcelain to grind and wash enamels.

Quills
Goose quills, from calligraphers' suppliers, are used to apply wet enamel.

Rolling mill
Use to impress textured designs on sheet silver for *champlevé* enamel.

Sieves (strainers)
Use to apply dry enamel. Match the size of the mesh to that of the ground enamel fragments.

Soldering equipment
You need solder, charcoal, a gas blowtorch and borax-based flux (auflux).

Tongs and tweezers
Brass or plastic tongs or tweezers must be used to move metal in and out of pickle or etchants.

Enamelling involves high temperatures and hazardous substances. Work in a well-ventilated place, wear protective clothing, follow all manufacturers' instructions and turn off the kiln when not needed.

Enamelling Techniques

Preparation of Metal

Metal must be degreased and de-oxidized (pickled) before enamelling. To make it more malleable, anneal it by heating with a blowtorch to cherry-red. Allow it to return to black then quench in cold water and pickle to remove oxidation.

1 To degrease, abrade metal with emery paper. Treat copper by placing in a general pickle solution (a 10% solution of sulphuric acid, safety pickle or alum).

2 Cover sterling or Britannia silver in neat nitric acid and swill gently until the metal appears white. (Fine silver does not need de-oxidizing.)

3 Brighten all metals with a brass brush and washing-up (dishwashing) liquid solution. Dry on a clean cotton cloth, taking care not to touch the area to be enamelled with your fingers.

Soldering

When designing a piece, aim to have as little soldering as possible under enamelling, to avoid the enamel discolouring or bubbling. During soldering, support the work with binding wire or tweezers if necessary, so that the sections do not move while you work.

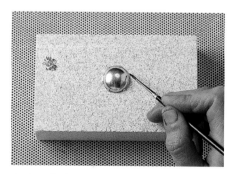

1 Apply borax-based flux (auflux) to the joint. Cut a length of solder into small pieces and apply them to the joint using a brush laden with flux.

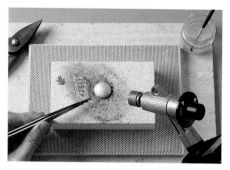

2 Play a flame over the whole piece to dry the flux without letting it bubble. When it is crystalline, direct the flame on the joint to heat both sides evenly until the solder melts.

3 Cool the piece then immerse in general pickle solution to remove fire stain and flux. Rinse the metal under running water, dry and remove any excess solder using a file.

Acid Etching

After metal has been pickled and brightened, the surface can be etched ready to take enamel. Wear protective gloves and goggles when working with etchants, and use only brass or plastic tweezers.

1 To protect the back and edges of the prepared metal from the etchant, paint on three coats of stopping-out varnish. Leave to dry.

2 Paint the design on the front in varnish. The acid will etch away any areas that are not covered by varnish. Alternatively, cover the whole surface then remove the varnish from areas to be etched using a fine steel point.

3 Place the piece in a solution of 1 part neat nitric acid to 3 parts cold water in an open plastic container. Stroke away bubbles using a feather. Remove the piece when the required depth of etching is achieved (not more than one-third of the thickness of the metal).

4 Rinse the metal under running water, using a glass fibre brush to clean off the etchant. Remove any remaining varnish with brush cleaner and brighten the surface by cleaning with a brass brush and washing-up (dishwashing) solution.

Photo-etching

Instead of painting the design on the metal, you can create a resist photographically. Draw a high-contrast black and white design, twice final size, with all lines at least 0.7mm/0.03in thick. (The black areas represent the metal and the white the enamelled areas.) Reduce the design to actual size on a photocopier.

Photocopy the reduced image at high contrast on a sheet of PnP blue acetate film, emulsion side up. Iron the resist on to the prepared metal, using a cotton/dry iron setting, to fix the image. Paint the back and edges of the piece with stopping-out varnish and etch with nitric acid as above.

Preparing Enamel

Intricate designs and curved surfaces usually require the enamel to be more finely ground than large, flat pieces. To start, break up enamel nuggets by wrapping them in a cotton cloth and hitting with a hammer.

1 In a clean mortar, cover a small piece of enamel with purified water and hit it with the pestle until it resembles granulated sugar. Add another piece and repeat until you have enough for your project, adding water to cover if necessary.

2 Hold the pestle upright and grind firmly with a circular action until the enamel feels soft and powdery. Allow to settle, then pour off the water. Rinse until the water runs clear and the enamel is uniform in colour.

Wet Application of Enamel

Pour the rinsed enamel into a palette and keep covered with water. It should be applied in several thin layers rather than one thick one, using a fine artist's brush, goose quill or stainless-steel point.

1 Pour off excess water and tip the palette so the waterline lies across the enamel. Pick up the enamel from just above the water. Apply evenly to the metal, pushing it well into any corners as it will draw back during firing.

2 Draw off any excess water by touching the edge of the metal with a clean cotton cloth. Do not touch the enamel itself as this will impair the finish of the fired surface. Fire the piece as soon as possible.

Dry Application of Enamel

Once the enamel is ground and cleaned, pour off as much water as possible then spread the paste on cooking foil, cover and leave to dry on top of the kiln or a radiator.

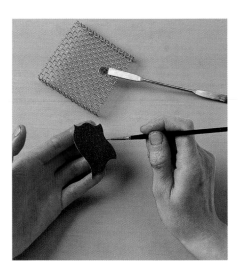

1 Having prepared the metal by degreasing and de-oxidizing it, cover the area to be enamelled with a layer of enamel gum, applying it thinly with a brush. Place it on a sheet of paper.

2 Place the enamel powder in a sieve (strainer), hold it about 5cm/2in above the metal and tap gently. Lift the metal and clean any excess enamel from the sides with a fine brush. Place the piece on a trivet ready for firing.

3 On subsequent layers, if you wish, you can paint a design in the enamel gum, or use a stencil, before sifting the enamel. Alternatively, you can scratch a design in the enamel before firing, using a paintbrush or steel point.

Kiln Firing The temperature of the kiln should be about 900°C/1,650°F for small items. Place the piece to be fired near the kiln to remove any moisture. Put it in the kiln when the surface looks crystalline and no more steam rises.

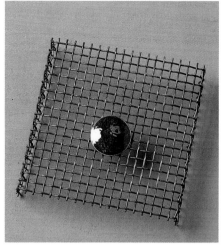

1 The enamel will lighten when it is first placed in the kiln and the metal will oxidize. Later the enamel will darken, still appearing matt (flat) and granular.

2 The enamel will then start to melt and look uneven but shiny.

3 Fully fired enamel looks smooth and shiny. If it pulls away from the edges and discolours, then it is overfired. It is best to underfire the first layers slightly and keep the highest firing for the last.

Finishing In order to achieve a smooth finish, the enamel needs to be abraded and polished after it has been fired. Depending on the shape of the piece you can use carborundum stones, diamond-impregnated paper or silicon carbide (wet and dry) paper, all of which are readily available in a range of grades.

1 Abrade the enamel using plenty of water and working in all directions. The surface will appear matt, showing up any low spots that may need to be filled with enamel and re-fired. Remove the residue with a glass fibre brush and water. Dry with a cotton cloth and do not touch the surface.

2 Re-fire the piece. When it is cool, place in a general pickle solution. Polish the enamel and metal with a paste of pumice powder and water, using a felt polishing mop either by hand or using a polishing motor running at 900–1200 rpm.

Fine wire and metal foils can be obtained from craft suppliers as well as hardware stores, but look out for containers such as oil cans and other unusual sources of metal that you can recycle.

Sheet Metal and Wirework Materials

Brass shim

Thin brass sheet is available in a range of thicknesses, as flat sheets or in rolls.

Copper wire

Soft copper wire has an attractive, warm colour and is easy to work with. It is available in a wide range of gauges and different tempers (hardnesses).

Epoxy resin glue

Strong, two-part glue can be used to join small sections of metal and items such as brooch backs.

Galvanized wire

A coating of zinc on steel wire prevents it rusting. Galvanized wire is springy and fairly hard to bend in thicker gauges.

Paints

Use hardwearing enamel paints to add bright, opaque colours to pieces of metal jewellery.

Pipe cleaners and paper clips (fasteners)

These quirky wire products are fun to work with. Both are available in many different colours and styles.

Silver-plated copper wire

This pretty wire is particularly well suited to jewellery making.

Solder

This is designed to melt and then harden to form a joint between pieces of metal. You should therefore always use a solder that has a lower melting point than the metals you are joining, and various alloys are available.

Tin plate

This is mild sheet steel coated with tin to stop it tarnishing. Biscuit tins are a useful source of recycled tin plate.

Wired tape

This thin, flat plastic tape with a wire core is designed for household and garden use and is available in various colours, such as green for tying plants.

Zinc sheet

Thin zinc sheet has a matt (flat) surface and is fairly soft and easy to cut.

You may already have many of the tools you will need as they are fairly basic. For coiling and shaping wire accurately it is essential to invest in some good pliers.

Sheet Metal and Wirework Equipment

Bench vice

Use a vice to clamp pieces of metal to a workbench or table when filing, drilling and hammering edges.

Centre punch

Use a punch or nail (with a hammer) to make decorative holes in metal.

File

A hand file can be used to remove burrs of metal from the edges after cutting out a shape from sheet metal.

Hammer

A medium ball hammer is used with a punch or nail to decorate tin plate, or alone to create a hammered texture.

Pliers

Use round-nosed (snub-nosed) or half-round pliers to coil wire, and parallel (channel-type) pliers to flatten coils.

Protective clothes

Heavyweight gloves and a thick work shirt should always be worn when working with metal.

Silicon carbide (wet and dry) paper

Damp fine-grade paper is good for finishing filed metal edges. Wrap the paper around a small wooden block.

Soldering iron

A soldering iron is used to heat solder when joining pieces of metal. The job should always be done on a fireproof soldering mat.

Tin snips

These are very strong shears, designed especially for cutting metal. They are available with either straight or curved blades (the latter type are used to cut curves and circles more easily).

Wire cutters

Always choose wire cutters that have good leverage. Don't be tempted to use scissors to cut wire as it will ruin their blades.

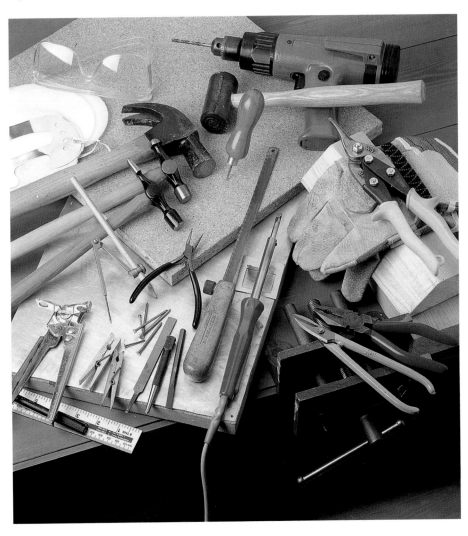

Neat wire coils and twists will make all the difference to the appearance of your finished pieces. Practise on a few spare lengths of wire to get the feel of your tools and the tension required.

Wirework Techniques

Making Coils

The coil is the most commonly used decorative device in wirework. If you are making a symmetrical ornament it will take some practice to create open coils of matching sizes.

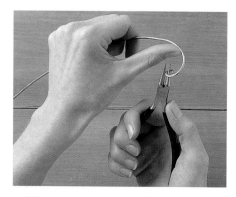

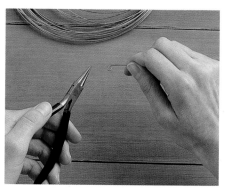

1 Using a pair of round-nosed (snub-nosed) pliers, make a small loop at the end of the wire. Hold the loop in the pliers, place your thumb against the wire and draw the wire across it to form a curve. Hold the pliers still and use your thumb to supply the tension needed as you bend the wire down.

2 After the first round has been formed, hold the middle of the coil flat with parallel (channel-type) pliers and continue to pull the wire round in a curve with your other hand. Use your eye to judge the space between the remaining turns of the coil.

3 Begin a closed coil in the same way as an open coil, by making a small loop in the end of the wire.

4 Hold the loop securely with parallel pliers and keep bending the wire around it, adjusting the position of the pliers as you work, until the coil is the required size.

Twisting Soft Wire

A hand drill can be used to twist soft wire neatly and quickly. You can use wires with different finishes and twist multiple strands in this way.

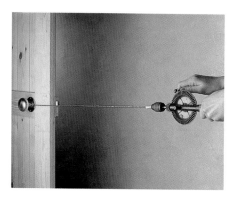

◀ Double the length of wire and loop it around a door handle. Wrap the ends in masking tape and secure them in the chuck of the drill. Keep the wire taut as you rotate the drill. Start slowly so that you can gauge the tension needed and continue until the wire is twisted to the degree required.

Thin sheet metal is not difficult to work with but the edges can be sharp, and tools such as tin snips and soldering irons should be treated with respect. Always wear protective clothing, even for small projects.

Sheet Metal Techniques

Cutting Metal

The cutting of any sheet metal produces small razor-sharp shards. Collect up these scraps as you go and keep them all together so that you can dispose of them safely when you have finished.

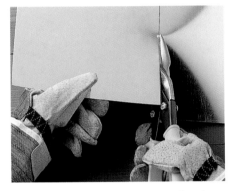

1 To avoid creating jagged edges, never close the blades of the shears completely. Keep the blades in the cut until the line is complete.

2 When cutting a curved shape, don't attempt to turn tin shears or snips: cut as much as you can then turn the metal to continue.

3 Large cans provide an excellent source of tin plate. Use a hacksaw blade to make a cut just below the top so that you are able to insert a blade of the tin snips and then cut around the drum. Cut straight down the side, then around the base, pushing back the panel as you go.

Finishing Edges

The cut edges of a piece of sheet metal are very sharp and should be smoothed immediately to prevent them causing harm to you or anyone else.

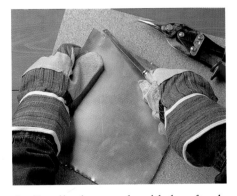

1 Small shapes should be firmly clamped in a vice for filing. Smooth all edges using a hand file, moving the file forwards at a right angle to the metal in one light stroke, then lifting it to repeat.

2 After the rough edges have been filed, make them completely smooth by finishing with fine-grade silicon carbide (wet and dry) paper. Dampen the paper and wrap it around a small sanding block.

This stylized – and stylish – bird, who carries a heart in his beak, is enamelled on silver to make an attractive lapel pin. In this project, the opaque enamel colours create a matt (flat) surface.

Bird Lapel Pin

you will need

tracing paper and pencil

double-sided tape

16 gauge/1.3mm/0.05in silver sheet

piercing saw

drill

silver tube and wire (inner diameter of tube to match thickness of wire)

soldering equipment

hard solder

pliers

burnisher

pestle and mortar

opaque enamels: white, bright red and mid-blue

black transparent enamel

enamel gum

glass fibre brush

trivet

fine artist's brush or quill

kiln and firing equipment

diamond-impregnated paper

fine-grade silicon carbide (wet and dry) paper

nail buffer

epoxy resin glue

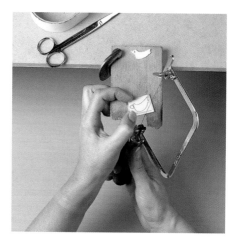

1 Trace the template at the back of the book. Stick the tracing on to the silver sheet using double-sided tape and cut out with a piercing saw. Drill a hole so that you can thread the saw blade through to reach the area between the heart and the bird.

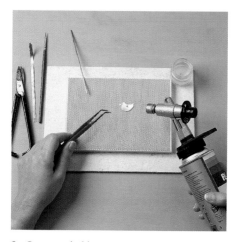

2 Cut and file a piece of silver tube 5mm/¼in long. Solder it in an upright position on to the back, using hard solder. For the pin, cut a 6cm/2½in length of silver wire. Bend with pliers 5mm/¼in in from one end to make a right angle.

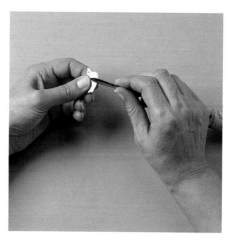

3 Burnish the edges of the bird to provide a "grip" for the enamel to adhere to. Grind and clean the enamels then add a drop of enamel gum to each and water to cover.

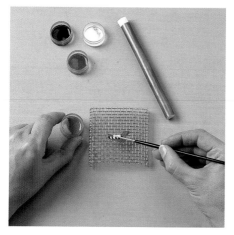

4 Degrease the silver using a glass fibre brush and water. Place the bird on a trivet and apply the enamel using a paintbrush or quill.

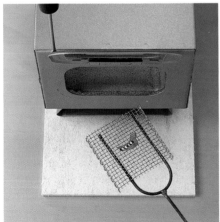

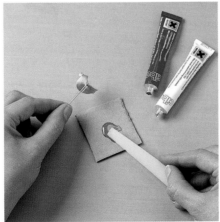

5 Place the bird on top of the kiln to dry, then fire it. Apply two more layers of enamel, firing each layer.

6 Abrade the enamel with diamond-impregnated paper and water. Smooth with damp silicon carbide paper and rinse. Leave the enamel surface matt (flat). Buff the plain silver side of the bird. Glue the pin into the tube using epoxy resin glue.

Embellish a variety of enamelled silver beads with tiny scraps of gold foil for a really opulent effect. Instead of a chain, you could thread a few beads on to a leather thong or a silk cord.

Gold Foil Beads

you will need

selection of silver beads

18 gauge/1mm/0.04in silver wire

scissors

metal rod of diameter to match holes in beads

piercing saw

soldering equipment

hard solder

pliers

glass fibre brush

trivet

pestle and mortar

turquoise transparent enamel

enamel gum

fine artist's paintbrush or quill

kiln and firing equipment

diamond-impregnated paper

gold foil

nail buffer

necklace chain

assorted silver and semi-precious beads

necklace findings and clasp

easy solder or epoxy resin glue

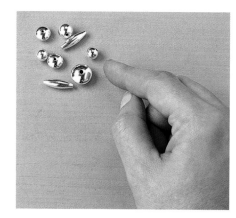

1 Assemble a collection of silver beads in different shapes and sizes to add interest to the necklace.

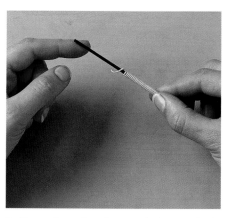

2 Cut a length of annealed round silver wire. Spiral it around a metal rod of the same diameter as the holes in the beads.

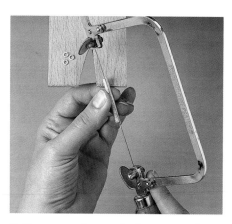

3 Remove the rod then cut down the length of the spiral, using a piercing saw, to make jump rings. Bend the rings to close the join and solder with hard solder.

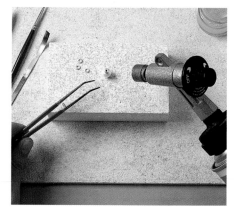

4 Using hard solder, solder a jump ring around the hole at the top and bottom of each bead. Remove the firestain and rinse, then clean the beads with a glass fibre brush and water.

  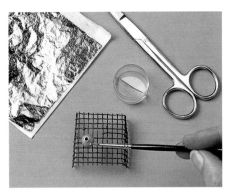

5 Cut and bend a piece of wire up from the trivet and place a bead on it to hold it during enamelling. Grind and clean the enamel then add a few drops of enamel gum and water to cover. Using the wet enamel as dry as possible, apply it to the bead with a fine paintbrush or quill. Dry out the enamelled beads on top of the kiln.

6 Fire the beads in the kiln. Repeat with two more layers of enamel, firing each layer. Abrade the enamel smooth with diamond-impregnated paper and water. Rinse.

7 Cut up small pieces of gold foil into geometric shapes with a pair of sharp scissors. Now, using a fine paintbrush dipped in a little enamel gum, attach these pieces of foil to some of the enamelled beads. Dry on top of the kiln and then fire.

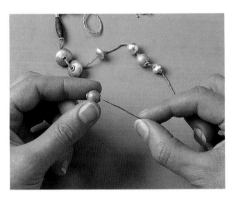

8 Polish the silver edges of the beads with a nail buffer. Thread on to the chain, mixing the enamelled beads with plain silver and semi-precious beads.

9 Attach the findings to the chain using easy solder. Solder or glue on the clasp. The clasp can be glued if using a leather thong or silk cord.

The subtle etched design resembling snakeskin on this handsome ring is enamelled in two shades of grey. Engrave a matching design around the side. The dimensions given here will make a medium to large ring.

Reptilian Ring

you will need

half-round jeweller's pliers

8.5mm/³⁄₈in x 5.8cm/2¼in strip of 12 gauge/2mm/0.08in silver, for the ring

soldering equipment

hard solder

general pickle solution

ring mandrel

mallet

file

emery paper

graver

17mm/²⁄₃in diameter circle of 18 gauge/1mm/0.04in silver, for the domed top

doming block

doming punch

drill

2mm/³⁄₃₂in x 6cm/2½in strip of 14 gauge/1.6mm/0.06in silver, for the bezel

2cm/³⁄₄in diameter circle of 18 gauge/1mm/0.04in silver, for the base

4mm/³⁄₁₆in square of 22 gauge/ 0.6mm/0.025in silver

14BA ³⁄₁₆th cheesehead brass screw and matching nut

stopping-out varnish

fine artist's paintbrush or quill

nitric acid

glass fibre brush

brush cleaner

brass brush

washing-up (dishwashing) liquid

easy solder

pumice powder

toothbrush

pestle and mortar

transparent enamels: mid-grey and dark grey

kiln and firing equipment

carborundum stone or diamond file

silicon carbide (wet and dry) paper

epoxy resin glue

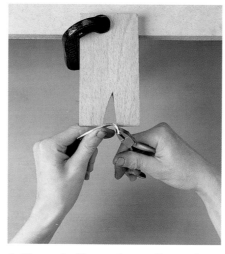

1 Using half-round jeweller's pliers, bend the strip of 12 gauge silver into a ring smaller than the finger size. Solder the joint, using hard solder. Pickle and rinse.

2 Check that the ring is circular by placing it on the mandrel and correcting it with a mallet. File, then sandpaper inside and out.

3 File the sides parallel. Scribe a light centre guideline around the outside. With the joint at the top, file a taper on both sides from a width of 8.5mm/³⁄₈in at the bottom to 4mm/³⁄₁₆in at the top. Engrave a reptilian design around the outside, using a graver, or etch with acid.

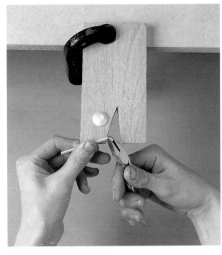

4 For the top, place the annealed 17mm/²⁄₃in silver circle in the doming block. Using a doming punch and a mallet, tap into a hemispherical shape.

5 Mark the centre of the domed top and drill a small hole to take the decorative brass screw.

6 Using the half-round-nosed pliers, bend the strip of 14 gauge silver into a collar, or bezel, so that it will fit snugly around the base of the domed top. Now solder the joint with hard solder. Check that the shape of the bezel is a circle on the ring mandrel, as described in step 2.

7 Solder the 2cm/³⁄₄in circle of silver to the bezel with hard solder to make the base. File the edge of the circle flush with the bezel, then file both to create an angled profile. Drill a 1mm hole through the centre of the 4mm/³⁄₁₆in silver square, then dome it to match the profile of the domed top. Thread the brass screw through the hole from the top and secure with hard solder underneath. File the top of the screw to make a decorative feature.

8 Clean and degrease the silver. Apply stopping-out varnish to the back, edges and hole of the domed top. Leave to dry, then paint a reptilian design in varnish on the front. Place in nitric acid diluted with 3 parts water for 3–3½ hours to etch the design. Rinse with water and a glass fibre brush and remove any remaining varnish with brush cleaner. Brighten the top using a brass brush and washing-up liquid solution.

9 Solder the bezel to the narrowest point of the ring strip at the joint, using easy solder. File and sand then apply pumice powder with a toothbrush. Brighten the silver with a glass fibre brush and washing-up liquid solution.

▶

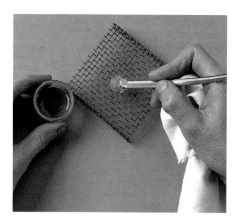

10 Grind and clean the enamels. Wet-apply the mid-grey enamel to the entire top surface, checking that it does not run into the hole. Fire in the kiln and leave to cool. On the next three to four layers, emphasize the etched recesses with dark-grey enamel to suggest scales. Use mid-grey for the rest of the design.

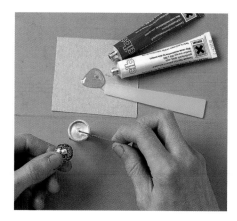

11 Use a carborundum stone or diamond file and silicon carbide paper to abrade the enamel. Use a glass fibre brush to rinse under running water, then fire for the final time. When cool, scrub with a paste of pumice powder and a toothbrush. Thread the decorative brass screw through the central hole of the dome and secure using the 14BA nut. Glue into the bezel using epoxy resin glue.

Wet-applying enamel on round objects is easier if it is ground very finely and you control the amount of water carefully. For a frosted finish, place the beads in matting salts for 2–3 minutes before pickling.

Striped Necklace

you will need

dividers

50cm/20in length of thick-walled, silver joint tubing, 4mm/³⁄₁₆in diameter

square or triangular needle file or lathe

piercing saw with fine blade

tube cutter or pin vice

file

silicon carbide (wet and dry) paper

ball fraize

copper or silver wire

brass brush

washing-up (dishwashing) liquid

pestle and mortar

transparent enamels

stainless steel wire

fine artist's paintbrush or quill

clean cotton cloth

kiln and firing equipment

diamond file or carborundum stone

general pickle solution

nylon thread and beading needle or fine silver chain

co-ordinating beads (optional)

necklace clasp

1 Using dividers, mark unequal stripes at random along the silver tubing.

2 Using a needle file, carefully make straight-sided grooves around the circumference of the tubing to a depth of 0.3mm. Try to keep them as even in depth as possible. Alternatively, turn the grooves on a lathe.

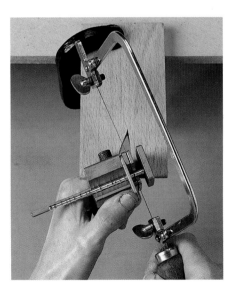

3 Using a piercing saw, carefully cut off unequal lengths of silver tubing between the recesses to make the actual beads. ▶

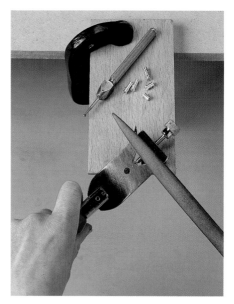

4 File the ends of each bead and smooth with silicon carbide paper. Countersink the central hole of each bead using a ball fraize.

5 Temporarily thread several beads on to a loop of wire and scrub with a brass brush and washing-up liquid solution.

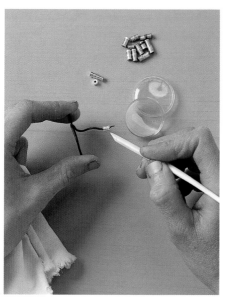

6 Grind the enamels very finely. Make several stainless-steel wire spirals to hold each bead firmly, as shown. Wet-apply the enamel, using a fine artist's paintbrush or quill. Draw off excess water with a clean cloth before firing.

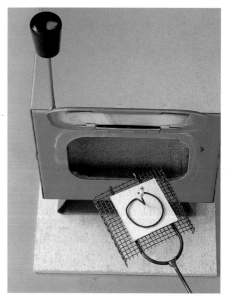

7 Keeping each bead on its wire spiral, fire in the kiln and leave to cool, still on the wire. Apply further layers of the same colour until each recess is full. Fire between each layer of enamel.

8 Thread each bead on a cranked length of stainless steel. Abrade each bead and smooth with silicon carbide paper, rotating the wired bead. Temporarily thread several beads on to a length of copper or silver wire. Rinse before and after pickling.

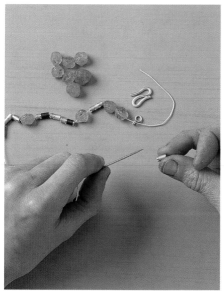

9 String the enamelled beads, perhaps interspersing them with co-ordinating beads. Alternatively, thread them on their own on to a fine silver chain. Attach a clasp.

Create your own design for these earrings, using transparent enamels in pale, clear colours. The holes should be large enough to allow the light to shine through but small enough to hold the wet enamel.

Plique-à-jour Earrings

you will need

pencil and paper

16 gauge/1.2mm/0.05in silver sheet

piercing saw

drill

tweezers

brass brush

washing-up (dishwashing) liquid

pestle and mortar

transparent enamels in pale colours

fine artist's paintbrush

trivet

kiln and firing equipment

sheet of mica (optional)

diamond-impregnated paper

pumice powder

jeweller's rouge

earring wires

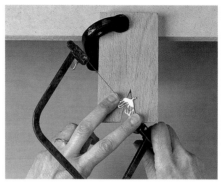

1 Draw your design on paper and attach it to the silver sheet. Using a piercing saw, cut out the shapes. Drill holes where the enamel will appear, then insert the saw into each hole and cut out. Use the saw to smooth the edges from front and back.

2 Shape the silver with a pair of tweezers. Clean the silver with a brass brush and washing-up liquid solution. Grind and wash the transparent enamels.

3 Using a fine paintbrush, apply the wet enamel into the spaces in the earrings. Practise getting the right consistency – if the enamel is too wet, it will fall through the holes.

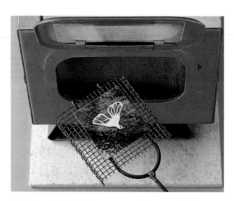

4 Fire while the enamel is still damp. Beginners may find it easier to fire on a sheet of mica. Remove from the kiln as soon as the enamel begins to melt. Refill the holes if the enamel has pulled to the side, and re-fire.

5 When the holes are completely filled, abrade the earrings with diamond-impregnated paper. Rinse and fire again. Polish with pumice powder and water, then jeweller's rouge. Attach the earring wires.

A central band of enamel with a simple photo-etched design makes an elegant decoration for this silver ring. You can omit the final firing if you would prefer a matt (flat) finish to the enamel.

Banded Ring

you will need

silver ring blank

PnP blue acetate film and iron

ring clamp

file

emery paper

pliers

binding wire

soldering equipment

hard solder

general pickle solution

ring mandrel

wooden or hide mallet

nitric acid

brass brush

washing-up (dishwashing) liquid

pestle and mortar

transparent enamels

enamel gum

fine artist's paintbrush or quill

kiln and firing equipment

diamond-impregnated paper

pumice powder or felt

polishing mop

1 Photocopy the template provided at the back of the book to produce a high contrast black-and-white design for photo-etching on to the ring blank (see Enamelling Techniques section). Place the ring blank in a clamp and shorten it to the required finger size by filing the ends. Smooth the sides with a file and then emery paper.

2 Using a pair of pliers, carefully bend in the ends to form a ring. The shape doesn't need to be perfectly round at this stage. Now file the ends of the ring so that they will meet exactly and make a good joint.

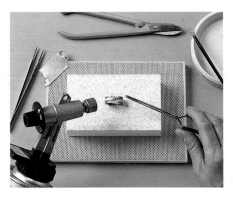

3 Twist binding wire around the ring. Solder the joint with hard solder, then quench in cold water and dry. Remove the wire, then pickle the ring.

4 File off the excess solder. Place the ring on a ring mandrel and tap with a mallet until it is perfectly round. Remove firestain by placing the ring in nitric acid, and then rinse. Now, using a brass brush, brush the silver with water and washing-up liquid solution until it is shiny.

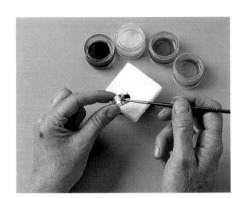

5 Grind and clean the enamels, then add a drop of enamel gum and water to cover. Apply carefully to the etched band using either a fine paintbrush or a quill. Leave the enamel to dry, then fire in the kiln. Now leave to cool.

6 Using medium-grade diamond-impregnated paper and water, abrade the enamel until you expose the silver design. Rinse the ring and apply more enamel to any shiny areas of the design then repeat the firing and abrading. Polish with fine-grade diamond-impregnated paper, rinse then fire again to glaze the surface if you wish. Leave to cool then pickle, rinse and polish the ring.

Choose transparent enamels in watery colours for these fish, set against a deep blue sea. The photo-etched design needs to be reversed for the second blank so that the cufflinks make a symmetrical pair.

Fishy Cufflinks

you will need

silver cufflink blanks to fit the template
or 17 gauge/1.1mm/0.045in
silver sheet
PnP blue acetate film and iron
piercing saw
ring clamp
file
emery stick (board)
wooden doming block
wooden doming punch
mallet
nitric acid
brass brush
washing-up (dishwashing) liquid
pestle and mortar
transparent enamels
enamel gum
fine artist's paintbrush or quill
trivet
kiln and firing equipment
diamond-impregnated paper
emery paper
soldering equipment
easy solder
cufflink findings
general pickle solution
pumice powder or felt polishing mop
(optional)

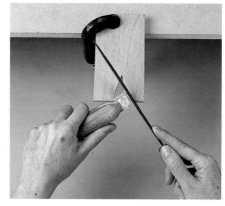

1 Photocopy the template at the back of the book to produce a high contrast black-and-white design. This needs to be photo-etched on to the cufflink blanks or silver sheet (see Enamelling Techniques section). Cut out the cufflink shapes with a piercing saw, place each one in a clamp and file the edges straight. Polish the edges with a fine emery stick.

2 Place each cufflink in the doming block. Tap the silver with a doming punch and mallet to create the desired domed shape.

3 De-oxidize the silver by placing each piece in nitric acid for a few minutes and then rinsing in cold water. Using a brass brush, scrub with washing-up liquid solution until the metal is shiny.

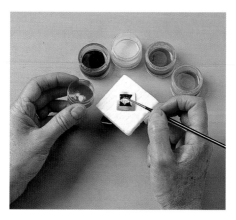

4 Grind and clean the enamels and add a drop of enamel gum to each. Apply the wet enamels to the design, using a paintbrush. Do not mix the colours. Leave to dry, then fire in the kiln until molten. Leave to cool.

5 Using a medium-grade diamond-impregnated paper and some water, abrade the enamel to expose the silver design, and then rinse. Apply more enamel and repeat. Polish with fine-grade paper, then fire again. Leave to cool. Remove the oxidation with emery paper.

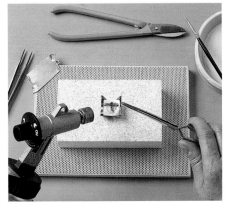

6 Melt easy solder on to the foot of each finding and solder to the back of the cufflink. Cool, then pickle and polish the cufflinks.

The design for these jolly earrings is transferred to a pair of silver blanks using the photo-etching technique. Remember to apply it to the second earring in reverse so that the finished pieces are symmetrical.

Stargazer Earrings

you will need

silver earring blanks, to fit the template,
or 17 gauge/1.1mm/0.045in
silver sheet
PnP blue acetate film and iron
piercing saw
ring clamp
file
fine emery stick (board)
masking tape
centre punch
drill
wooden doming block
wooden doming punch
mallet
nitric acid
brass brush
washing-up (dishwashing) liquid
pestle and mortar
transparent enamels
enamel gum
fine artist's paintbrush or quill
trivet
kiln and firing equipment
diamond-impregnated paper
emery paper
general pickle solution
pumice powder or felt polishing mop
(optional)
earring wires
pliers

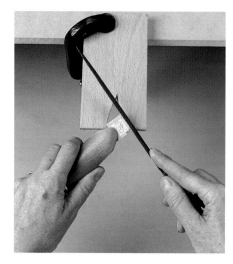

◄ **1** Photocopy the template provided at the back of the book to produce a high contrast black-and-white design the size of the finished earrings. This design needs to be photo-etched on to the earring blanks or silver sheet (see Enamelling Techniques section). Now cut out the earring shapes with a piercing saw, place each earring in a clamp and file the edges straight.

2 Polish the edges of the earrings with a fine emery stick to remove any scratch marks left after filing.

3 Secure each earring in turn on your work surface with masking tape. Centre punch and drill a hole in the top edge for the wires.

4 Place each earring in the doming block. Tap the silver with a doming punch and mallet to create the desired domed shape.

5 De-oxidize the earrings by placing them in nitric acid for a few minutes, then rinsing in cold water. Using a brass brush, brush with washing-up liquid solution until shiny. Hold by the edges only.

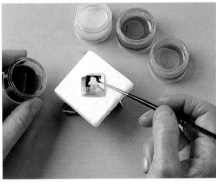

6 Grind and clean the enamels, then add a drop of enamel gum and water to cover. Apply the wet enamels, using a paintbrush or quill. Take care not to mix the colours.

7 Leave the earrings to dry, then fire in the kiln until the enamel is molten. Leave to cool. Apply further layers of enamel and fire each time until the cells of the design appear full.

8 Using medium-grade diamond-impregnated paper and water, abrade the enamel until you expose the silver design. Apply more enamel to any shiny areas, then repeat the firing, abrading and rinsing. Refire to glaze the surface.

9 Leave to cool. Abrade the back of the earrings with emery paper, and then place in pickle solution to remove oxidation.

10 Polish both sides of the earrings if desired. Carefully open the ear wires with the jewellery pliers and insert through the drilled holes. Squeeze the wires gently together to close.

This jaunty character is created by photo-etching the design on to a square brooch, leaving a generous frame of silver, then filling the etching with enamel. Follow the colours shown here or choose your own.

Pet Brooch

you will need

silver brooch blank, to fit the template, or 17 gauge/
1.1mm/0.045in silver sheet

PnP blue acetate film and iron

piercing saw

ring clamp

file

fine emery stick (board)

wooden doming block

wooden doming punch

mallet

nitric acid

brass brush

washing-up (dishwashing) liquid

pestle and mortar

transparent enamels

enamel gum

fine artist's paintbrush or quill

trivet

kiln and firing equipment

diamond-impregnated paper

emery paper

soldering equipment

brooch catch, joint and pin

easy solder

pickle solution

toothbrush

pumice powder

parallel (channel-type) pliers

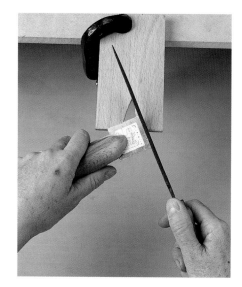

◀ **1** Photocopy the template at the back of the book to produce a high contrast black-and-white design. The design needs to be photo-etched on to the brooch blank or silver sheet (see Enamelling Techniques section) and the template should be copied at the actual size of the finished brooch. If you are using sheet silver, cut out the brooch shape with a piercing saw, place the silver in a clamp and file the edges straight.

2 Polish the edges of the brooch with a fine emery stick to remove any scratch marks left by the file.

3 Place the annealed brooch blank in the doming block. Tap lightly with the punch and mallet until the piece is slightly domed.

4 De-oxidize the silver by placing in nitric acid for a few minutes then rinsing in cold water. Using a brass brush, brush with water and washing-up liquid until shiny. Hold by the edges only.

5 Grind and clean the enamels, then add a drop of enamel gum and water to cover. Apply the wet enamels using a paintbrush or quill. Leave to dry on top of the kiln.

6 Fire in the kiln until the enamel is molten. Leave to cool. Apply further layers of enamel, firing in between each layer, until the cells appear full.

7 Using medium-grade diamond-impregnated paper and water, abrade the enamel until you expose the silver design. Apply more enamel to any shiny areas, then repeat the firing, abrading and rinsing. Refire to glaze the surface.

8 Leave to cool then remove the oxidation from the back of the brooch with emery paper.

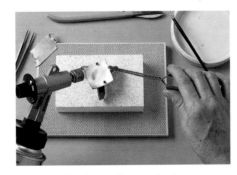

9 Place the brooch upside down on a trivet so that only the edges touch. Solder on the brooch catch and joint with easy solder. Leave to cool, then place in pickle solution. Rinse, then clean using a toothbrush and a paste of pumice powder.

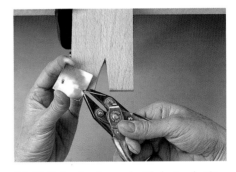

10 Polish the brooch if desired. Cut the brooch pin to length and place it in the ball joint. Using parallel pliers, squeeze the joint carefully to hold the pin in place.

Decorate this photo-etched pendant with as many transparent enamel colours as you like, including several shades of green, to evoke the atmosphere of a sunny summer garden in full bloom.

Flower Pendant

you will need

silver pendant blank, to fit the template, or 17 gauge/1.1mm/0.045in silver sheet

PnP blue acetate film and iron

piercing saw

ring clamp

file

emery stick (board)

wooden doming block

wooden doming punch

mallet

nitric acid

brass brush

washing-up (dishwashing) liquid

pestle and mortar

transparent enamels

enamel gum

fine artist's paintbrush or quill

trivet

kiln and firing equipment

diamond-impregnated paper

fine-grade emery paper

small piece of silver wire

soldering equipment

easy solder

tweezers

pickle solution

pumice powder or felt

polishing mop (optional)

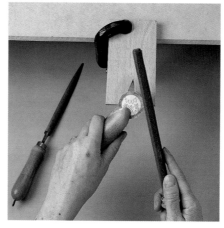

1 Photocopy the template at the back of the book to produce a high contrast black-and-white design. Photo-etch the design on to the silver. Cut out the shape with a piercing saw and file the edges until circular, then smooth with an emery stick.

2 Shape the pendant in a doming block, using a doming punch and mallet. To de-oxidize the silver, place it in nitric acid for a few minutes then rinse with water. Scrub with a brass brush and washing-up liquid solution.

3 Grind and clean the enamels, then add a drop of enamel gum to each and water to cover. Apply the wet enamels using a paintbrush or quill. Take care not to mix the colours. Leave to dry, then fire in the kiln. Leave to cool.

4 Using diamond-impregnated paper and water, abrade the enamel to expose the silver design, then rinse. Apply more enamel to the shiny areas, then repeat. Abrade the enamel and fire again.

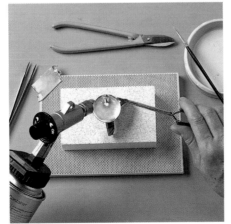

5 Leave to cool, then remove the oxidation from the back of the pendant by rubbing with fine-grade emery paper.

6 Bend the wire into a loop and melt easy solder on to the ends. To attach the loop to the pendant, hold it in tweezers against the back of the pendant and heat the ends until they join. Leave to cool, then pickle and polish the pendant as desired.

A delicately textured surface is created by impressing silver with watercolour paper then applying two enamel colours and flux to create a marbled effect. Small shards of silver foil are fired between the layers.

Shield Earrings

you will need

scissors

rough-textured watercolour paper

20 gauge/0.8mm/0.03in silver sheet

blowtorch

general pickle

rolling mill

tracing paper and pencil

double-sided tape

piercing saw

file

drill

burnisher

brass brush

washing-up (dishwashing) liquid

clean cotton cloth

pestle and mortar

transparent enamels: mauve and pale yellow-green

fine artist's paintbrush or quill

borax-based flux (auflux)

trivet

kiln and firing equipment

craft (utility) knife

scraps of fine silver foil

diamond file or carborundum stone

silicon carbide (wet and dry) paper

earring wires

round-nosed (snub-nosed) pliers

2 small domed silver discs

2 frosted beads

2 bead pins

1 Cut a piece of watercolour paper slightly larger than the silver sheet. Anneal the silver and remove the oxidation (see Enamelling Techniques section). Place the silver sheet on top of the paper and run them together through the rolling mill, with the rollers tightly clamped down.

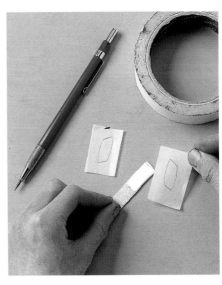

2 Trace the templates at the back of the book to create the main body of both earrings. Attach the tracings to the silver with double-sided tape.

3 Using a piercing saw, cut out the shield shapes. File the edges. Drill small holes in two matching diagonally opposed corners of each shield. ▶

4 Burnish around the sides to raise an edge to contain the enamel. Now scrub the shields with a brass brush and washing-up liquid solution, rinse and dry.

5 Grind and clean the enamels. Using a fine paintbrush or quill, wet-apply the flux and mauve enamel randomly to create a marbled effect. Ensure that they do not run into the drilled holes.

6 Draw off any excess water with a clean cotton cloth. Fire the first layer in the kiln and leave to cool.

7 Using a craft knife, cut small jagged pieces of silver foil. Moisten the fired enamel with water and apply the pieces of foil in a broken S-shaped line, using a damp paintbrush. Draw off any excess water with a cloth. Wet-apply a spot of flux to one corner of each shield and fire. When the flux has fused, the foil will have adhered to the enamel.

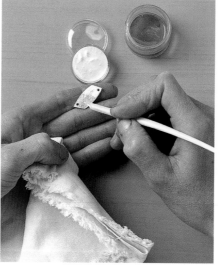

8 When cool, wet-apply the yellow-green enamel over the foil. Apply flux to all other areas and fire. Finally, fire a last layer using flux only.

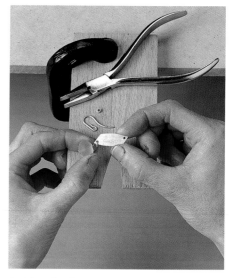

9 Abrade the fired surface using a diamond file, then rinse and fill in any low spots with more enamel, and re-fire. Remove excess enamel from the edges then finish all sides of the shields with fine-grade silicon carbide paper and rinse. Attach the earring wires to the holes at the top of the earrings and add discs, frosted beads and bead pins to the bottom.

This modern brooch is made in three layers, sandwiching copper between sheets of silver. The design is accentuated by stencil-rolling waves on the silver before enamelling to create a textured effect.

Wave Brooch

you will need

scissors

rough-textured watercolour paper

4 x 2.5cm/1$\frac{1}{2}$ x 1in piece of 18 gauge/ 1mm/0.04in silver sheet

pencil

craft (utility) knife

nitric acid

rolling mill

graver

tracing paper

4 x 6cm/1$\frac{1}{2}$ x 2$\frac{1}{2}$in piece of 18 gauge/1mm/0.04in copper sheet

piercing saw

scriber

4 x 6cm/1$\frac{1}{2}$ x 2$\frac{1}{2}$in piece of 20 gauge/0.8mm/0.03in silver sheet

file

drill

4 x 14BA $\frac{3}{16}$th cheesehead brass bolts and matching nuts

burnisher

glass fibre brush

washing-up (dishwashing) liquid

pestle and mortar

transparent enamels: turquoise and blue

fine artist's paintbrush or quill

flux

trivet

kiln and firing equipment

carborundum stone or diamond file

silicon carbide (wet and dry) paper

pumice powder

toothbrush

stopping-out varnish

brush cleaner

blowtorch

soldering equipment

hard solder

brooch catch, joint and pin

pickle solution

1 Cut the watercolour paper larger than the piece of 18 gauge silver sheet. Draw stylized wave shapes on the paper and cut out carefully with a craft knife to make a stencil.

2 Anneal the silver sheet. Remove the firestain by placing it in nitric acid until it whitens. Place the paper stencil on top of the sheet. Run them together through the rolling mill, with the rollers tightly clamped down. Emphasize the waves by engraving a few lines around them with a graver.

3 Trace template 1 from the back of the book on to the copper sheet and cut out with a piercing saw. Using a scriber, draw round this shape on to the 20 gauge silver sheet. ▶

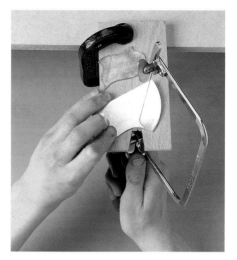

4 Cut out the silver just outside the marked line so that it is slightly larger than the copper shape. Next, trace template 2 on to the rolled, textured silver and cut out. File the edges of all the pieces.

5 Drill a small hole in each corner of the rolled silver to fit the brass screws. Burnish the edges to provide a lip to contain the enamel. Scrub thoroughly with a glass fibre brush and washing-up liquid solution, and then rinse.

6 Grind and clean the enamels. Wet-apply the turquoise enamel, using a paintbrush or quill. Make sure it does not flow into the holes. Fire this layer.

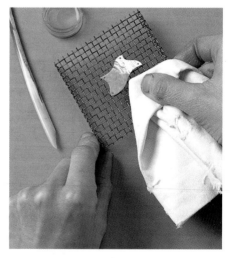

7 For the next three to four layers of enamel, emphasize the wavy lines by shadowing with blue and highlighting them with the flux, applied with a clean, dry cloth.

8 Abrade the fired enamel using a carborundum stone or diamond file. Rinse, fill in low spots and re-fire if necessary. Abrade again, smooth with silicon carbide paper, then scrub with a glass fibre brush under running water. Scrub the back and sides with a paste of pumice powder and water, using a toothbrush.

9 Scrub the copper with pumice powder, then de-grease with a glass fibre brush and washing-up liquid solution. Cover the back and edges with stopping-out varnish and paint a "breezy" border on the front. When the varnish is dry, place the brooch in nitric acid diluted in 3 parts water for about 5 minutes. Rinse, then remove any varnish with brush cleaner. File the edges.

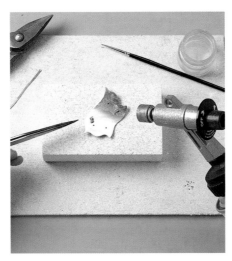

10 Gently shape the silver and copper backing pieces to match the curve of the enamelled piece. Colour the copper iridescent purple by gently heating it with a blowtorch. Drill holes in both pieces to match the enamelled piece.

11 Solder the brooch fittings on to the backing piece using hard solder. Pickle and rinse. Abrade thoroughly with silicon carbide paper, then with a toothbrush and pumice powder that has been mixed to a paste with water.

12 Clean with a glass fibre brush and washing-up liquid solution. Rivet the brooch pin. Assemble the brooch using brass screws and nuts.

In *cloisonné* work, fine wires are laid down in a pattern to make cells for the enamels. The triangles in this design echo the outline of the silver mounts, and small curls of silver wire add a final flourish.

Cloisonné Earrings

you will need

piercing saw

18 gauge/1mm/0.04in silver sheet

tracing paper and pencil

24 gauge/0.5mm/0.02in silver sheet

double-sided tape

file

fine emery stick (board)

metal snips

16 gauge/1.2mm/0.05in round silver wire

pliers

soldering equipment

hard solder

swage block

wooden doming punch

mallet

silver earring posts and backs

burnisher

glass fibre brush

scissors

28 gauge/0.3mm/0.013in silver cloisonné wire

fine artist's paintbrush

enamel gum

trivet

pestle and mortar

transparent enamels: turquoise, light amber, bright blue

quill (optional)

kiln and firing equipment

diamond-impregnated paper

silicon carbide (wet and dry) paper

nail buffer

1 Cut two 16 x 22mm/⅝ x ⅞in rectangles from the thicker silver sheet. To create the earring tops, trace template 1 from the back of the book. Attach the tracing to the thinner silver sheet with double-sided tape. Cut out twice, using a piercing saw.

2 File the two cut-out earring tops and smooth the edges with a fine emery stick. Cut two lengths of round silver wire and bend into matching curls with pliers, following the shape of templates 2 and 3.

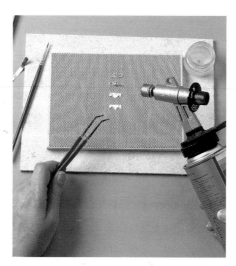

3 Melt hard solder on to the back of the earring tops and the straight part of the wire design.

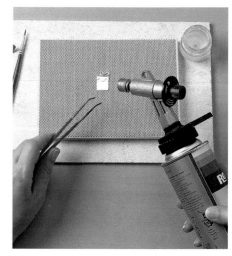

4 Position the earring tops and the wire designs, solder side down, in place on top of the silver rectangles. Flux the metal and rerun the solder with the blowtorch.

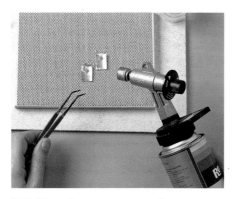

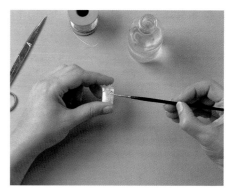

5 Place each earring face down in a swage block. Lay a wooden doming punch along its length and tap with a mallet to create a curved shape.

6 Solder the earposts to the earrings with hard solder. Burnish the edges of the earrings to provide a "grip" for the enamel to adhere to. Clean the metal with a glass fibre brush and water.

7 Cut the required lengths of *cloisonné* wire and lay on each earring in a geometric pattern, using a fine paintbrush dipped in a little enamel gum. Place on a trivet.

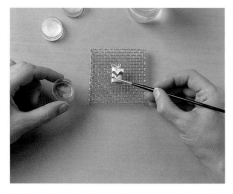

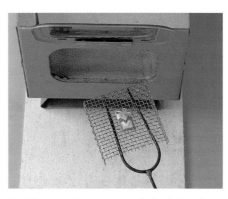

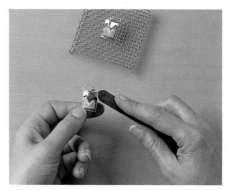

8 Grind and clean the enamels. Add a few drops of enamel gum and water to cover. Using a fine paintbrush or quill, apply the enamel to the cells between the *cloisonné* wires.

9 Allow to dry on top of the kiln, then fire. Apply two more layers of enamel, firing twice more. The enamel should now reach the top of the wire.

10 Abrade the enamel with diamond-impregnated paper and water to expose any covered *cloisonné* wire. Rinse and re-fire. Smooth the silver with silicon carbide paper and finish with a buffer.

In this brooch, the enamel is applied within *cloisonné* cells and is also enclosed within a wire rectangle, which acts as a frame. The piece shows how this traditional technique perfectly suits a modern design.

Cloisonné Brooch

you will need

metal snips

18 gauge/1mm/0.04in square silver wire

square needle file

soldering equipment

general pickle solution

hard solder

18 gauge/1mm/0.04in silver sheet

piercing saw

swage block

wooden doming punch

mallet

brooch catch, joint and pin

glass fibre brush

28 gauge/0.3mm/0.013in fine silver cloisonné wire

scissors

fine artist's paintbrush

enamel gum

pestle and mortar

transparent enamels: turquoise, black, grey and light amber

opaque enamel: bright red

quill (optional)

trivet

kiln and firing equipment

diamond-impregnated paper

silicon carbide (wet and dry) paper

nail buffer

parallel (channel-type) pliers

1 Cut two 5cm/2in lengths of 18 gauge square silver wire. Holding a square needle file at an angle, file a triangular groove 18mm/¾in from one end of each wire, three-quarters of the way through the wire's thickness. Anneal the wires (see Enamelling Techniques section), and bend to right angles at the filed points. Solder the mitre on each wire, using hard solder.

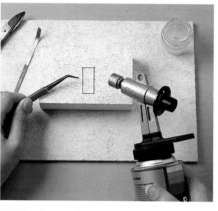

2 File the ends of the two L-shapes at 45° so that they will fit together to make a rectangular frame. Solder together with hard solder.

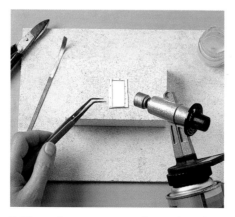

3 Place the wire rectangle on the silver sheet. Lay pieces of hard solder around the outside of the wire frame and solder it to the silver sheet. Cut off the excess silver sheet but do not file the edges until the enamelling is complete.

4 Place the piece in a swage block, with the side to be enamelled face down. Using a wooden punch and mallet, create a curved shape.

▶

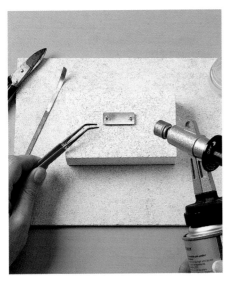

5 Solder the brooch fittings on to the back, using hard solder.

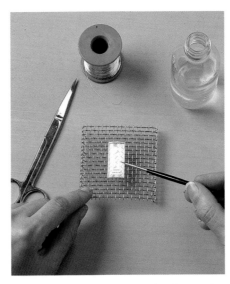

6 Remove firestain and clean the front of the brooch thoroughly with a glass fibre brush and water. Cut the *cloisonné* wire into the required lengths and place on the brooch to make the geometric pattern, using a fine paint-brush dipped in enamel gum.

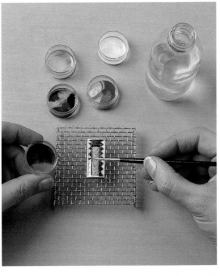

7 Grind and clean the enamels. Add a few drops of enamel gum to each colour, with water to cover. Using a fine artist's paintbrush or a quill, apply the enamel to the cells created by the *cloisonné* wires.

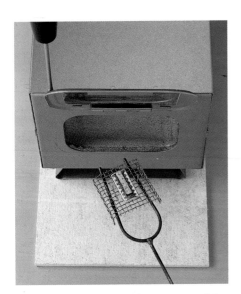

8 Leave the piece to dry on top of the kiln, then fire the enamel. Apply two more layers of enamel, firing each layer. The enamel should now reach the top of the wire.

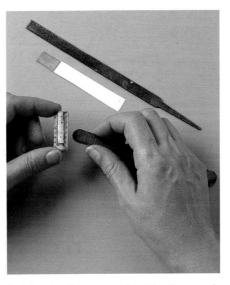

9 Abrade the enamel with diamond-impregnated paper and water until it is even, exposing any *cloisonné* wires that have been covered. Rinse thoroughly with water and a glass fibre brush and re-fire. File the silver around the outer edges of the brooch.

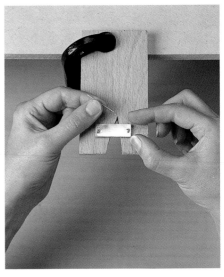

10 Clean and polish the edges of the silver with silicon carbide paper and a nail buffer. Attach the brooch pin using parallel pliers.

The slender elegant shape of this pendant is reminiscent of Art Deco jewellery. A little *cloisonné* detailing has been added within the delicate silver frame, matching its geometric design.

Triangular Pendant

you will need

tracing paper, pencil and ruler

24 gauge/0.5mm/0.02in silver sheet

double-sided tape

piercing saw

drill

file

soldering equipment

hard solder

18 gauge/1mm/0.04in silver sheet

swage block

wooden doming punch

mallet

doming block

silver chain

glass fibre brush

trivet

small, sharp scissors

28 gauge/0.3mm/0.013in fine silver cloisonné wire

fine artist's paintbrush

enamel gum

pestle and mortar

transparent enamels: turquoise, light amber, bright blue and grey

quill (optional)

kiln and firing equipment

diamond-impregnated paper

silicon carbide (wet and dry) paper

nail buffer

silver necklace clasp

1 Trace template 1 from the back of the book on to tracing paper. Attach the tracing to the 24 gauge silver sheet with double-sided tape.

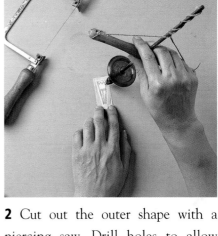

2 Cut out the outer shape with a piercing saw. Drill holes to allow access for the saw blade and cut out the inner parts of the design. File and smooth the inside edges.

3 Melt some small pieces of hard solder on to the back of the pierced pendant shape.

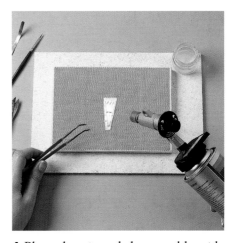

4 Place the pierced shape, solder side down, on the 18 gauge silver sheet. Place hard solder around the outside and solder the pierced shape to the sheet. If any solder runs into the areas that are to be enamelled, it should be removed.

▶

5 Following template 2, saw off the excess silver sheet, leaving a tab at the top for a loop and a circle at the bottom. Do not file the edges. Drill a hole in the centre of both tab and circle.

6 Place the pendant face down in a swage block. Using the doming punch on its side, tap it into a curved shape using a mallet.

7 Cut out a circle of silver sheet fractionally larger than the circle at the bottom of the pendant. Place in a doming block and create a small dome. File the base of the dome flat.

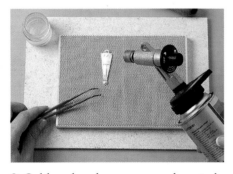

8 Solder the dome on to the circle at the bottom of the pendant with hard solder. Use a piercing saw to make the opening in the tab large enough to take your silver chain. Clean the metal with a glass fibre brush and water. Place on a trivet.

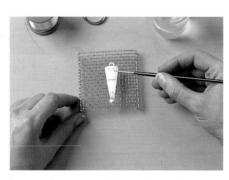

9 Cut the required lengths of *cloisonné* wire and place in the recesses in the pendant to form a geometric pattern, using a fine paintbrush dipped in enamel gum.

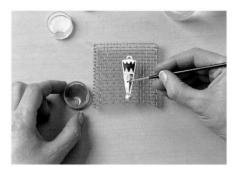

10 Grind and clean the enamels. Add a few drops of enamel gum and water to cover. Apply the enamel to the cells, using a fine paintbrush or quill.

11 Leave the enamel to dry on top of the kiln, then fire. Apply two more thin layers of enamel, firing each time.

12 Abrade the enamel with diamond-impregnated paper and water. Clean with a glass fibre brush and water. Refire. File the pendant edges. Smooth the silver areas with silicon carbide paper. Finish with a buffer. Thread the chain through the loop. Solder on a clasp and polish.

Adorn patch pockets with these highly original and decorative clips. Galvanized wire has been used here; if you wish, the wire can be sprayed with metallic car paint to change its colour.

Pocket Clips

you will need
wire cutters
18 gauge/1mm/0.04in and 22 gauge/
0.6mm/0.025in galvanized wire
ruler or tape measure
round-nosed (snub-nosed) pliers
half-round jeweller's pliers

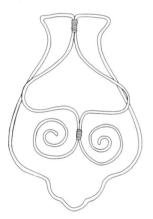

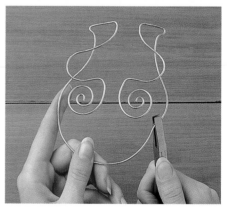

1 Cut a 1m/40in length of 18 gauge galvanized wire. Make a coil at one end with the round-nosed pliers. Bend the wire to make an S-shape, referring to the diagram above. Square off the loop below the coil with half-round pliers.

2 Using half-round pliers, nip in the wire to form one side of the neck, then make a large loop in the wire. From top to bottom the large loop measures 11.5cm/4½in. Make a mirror-image loop and coil on the other side of the large loop, cutting off any excess wire.

3 Fold the structure in half and bend the top of the large loop at both sides to make shoulders. Nip in the bottom of the large loop to make a scallop. Using the 22 gauge wire, bind the coils together and bind the neck for 12mm/½in.

This necklace is great fun to create and is the perfect project to make with children. You could also make matching accessories using clip-on earring backs and headband bases.

Furry Flower Necklace

you will need
round-nosed (snub-nosed) pliers
plain, furry and thick, bumpy
pipe cleaners
coloured paper clips (fasteners)
wired tape
wire cutters

1 Using round-nosed pliers, make small flowers from plain pipe cleaners. Make the centres of the flowers by straightening paper clips and coiling them into spirals. Bend a pipe cleaner into a five-petalled flower and twist the ends together.

2 Coil a plain pipe cleaner and a striped paper clip into a tight, neat spiral to make the centre of the largest flower. Tie a knot in a length of wired tape and thread it neatly through the flower centre so that the knot sits at the front.

3 Bend a thick, bumpy pipe cleaner to form the necklace. Bind the small flowers to the pipe cleaner necklace with the wired tape, tucking in the tape ends behind the flowers. Bind the large flower to a paper clip and clip on to the pipe cleaner necklace.

▲ **4** Form a loop at each end of the pipe cleaner. Attach wired tape to each loop. Coil two paper clips into cones and slide them on to the ends. Bend straightened paper clips into coils and join them together to make two chains. Attach the chains to the ends of the pipe cleaner. Make a "hook-and-eye" fastening from paper clips.

A good way to use up small scraps of tin is to make brooches. These can be simple in construction and made special with some painted decoration. Enamel paints are opaque and look stunning.

Painted Tin Brooch

you will need

30 gauge/0.25mm/0.01in tin sheet

felt-tipped pen

protective gloves

tin snips

bench vice

file

silicon carbide (wet and dry) paper

chinagraph pencil

enamel paints

fine paintbrushes

clear gloss polyurethane varnish

epoxy resin glue

brooch fastener

1 To make the brooch front, draw a circle 5cm/2in in diameter on a piece of tin with a marker pen. Now, making sure first that you are wearing protective gloves, cut out the circle using tin snips.

2 Clamp the tin circle in a bench vice and file the edges. Finish off the edges with damp silicon carbide paper so that they are smooth.

3 Draw a motif on one side of the brooch using a chinagraph pencil. Paint around the outline with enamel paint, then fill in the design. Leave the brooch to dry thoroughly.

4 Paint in the background, then add any features on top of the first coat of paint, using a fine paintbrush and enamel paint. Leave to dry. Seal the surface with two coats of clear gloss polyurethane varnish. Leave to dry thoroughly between coats.

5 Mix some epoxy resin glue and use it to stick a brooch fastener on to the back. Let the glue dry thoroughly before wearing the brooch.

Reproduce the delicate texture of a web in glittering copper and silver wire. The resident spider is resplendent in blue and gold and not at all threatening, especially as she has only six legs and a curly tail!

Spider's Web Brooch

you will need

18 gauge/1mm/0.04in copper wire

ruler

wire cutters

round-nosed (snub-nosed) pliers

22 gauge/0.6mm/0.025in silver wire

self-hardening clay

modelling tool

two small glass beads

brooch pin

epoxy resin glue

turquoise acrylic paint

paintbrush

clear varnish

gold powder

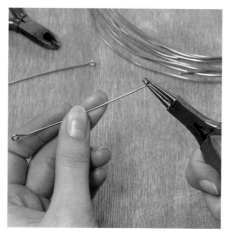

1 Cut four 7.5cm/3in lengths of copper wire. Curl both ends of each piece into a loop using round-nosed pliers.

2 Arrange the pieces to form a star. Wrap the silver wire round the centre. Working outwards in a spiral, twist the silver wire once round each copper wire. Secure and trim.

3 Cut six 6cm/2½in lengths of copper wire. Curl one end of each into a tight loop then bend the rest of the length into the shape of the spider's legs.

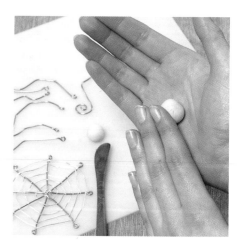

4 Cut a 7.5cm/3in length of wire and bend it into a spiral for the tail. Roll two balls of self-hardening clay for the body and head.

5 Press the two clay balls together, joining securely with the help of the modelling tool. Smooth the surface of the clay with wet fingers or the modelling tool.

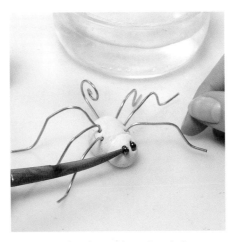

6 Insert the looped ends of the wire legs and tail into the spider's body. Press two glass beads into the head to make the eyes.

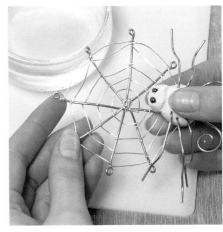

7 Press the spider's body on to the wire web. Flatten a small piece of clay and attach it to the spider from underneath the web, using the modelling tool to join it securely. Leave the clay to harden.

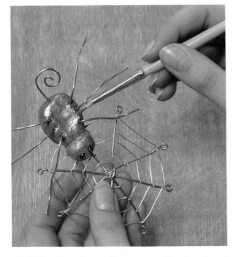

8 Glue the brooch pin to the back of the spider, and secure the legs and tail with drops of glue. Paint the body and head turquoise and leave to dry. Apply a coat of varnish to seal the paint. Mix gold powder with a little varnish and apply swiftly with a dry brush to leave some of the turquoise paint showing through.

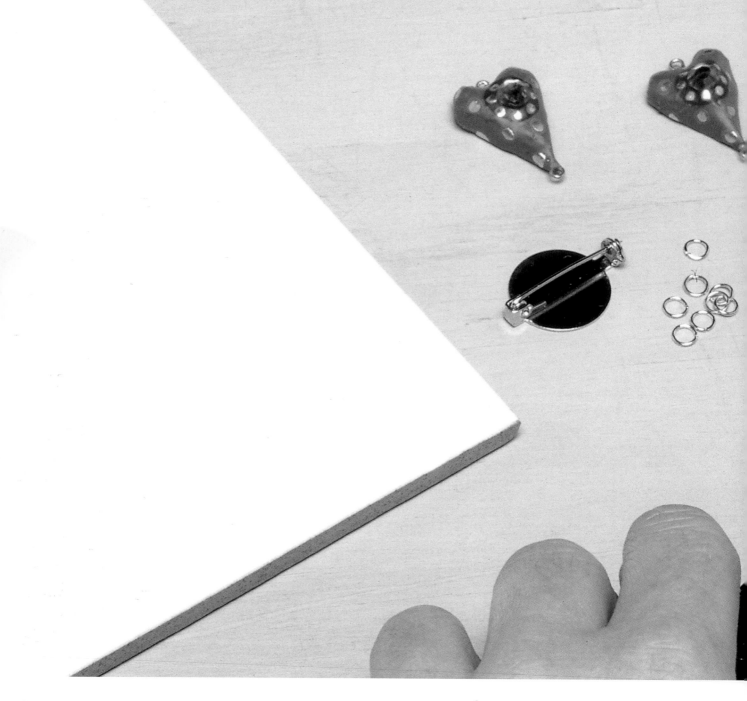

Paper, Card
and Wood

As a raw material, paper is both plentiful and adaptable. Turned into durable papier mâché it can be fashioned into beads, sculptural brooches or earrings, and intricate decoupage shapes make a fascinating decorative treatment for even the smallest of items. Wood can easily be cut and painted in imaginative ways to make bright, fun badges, or used to construct a beautiful box to hold all of your precious trinkets.

Gorgeous paper is easy to find in specialist stores, but look out for
unusual packaging, gift wraps and foils that can be recycled in your
jewellery projects, and collect pretty patterns for decoupage designs.

Paper and Card Materials

Cardboard

Double-walled corrugated cardboard
makes a firm base for papier mâché, but
for small items use stiff, thin card.
Single-walled corrugated cardboard is
flexible; use it to cover stylish boxes.

Foil

Buy gold, silver or coloured foil from
craft stores or use sweet (candy) papers.

Gift wrap

Printed wrapping paper is a good
source of decoupage images.

Glue

PVA (white) glue is ideal for sticking
paper and card. It can also be diluted
and used to soak newspaper for papier
mâché as an alternative to wallpaper
paste. Use strong epoxy resin glue to
attach jewellery findings to your
finished pieces.

Newspaper

Tear newspaper into thin strips
and soak in wallpaper paste or
dilute PVA (white) glue to make
papier mâché.

Paints

Gouache and acrylic paints dry
quickly and are easy to use. For
brilliant, glossy colour and sparkling
metallic effects, use enamel paint.

Papier mâché pulp

You can make papier mâché
pulp easily yourself (see Paper and
Card Techniques) or buy it ready-made
from craft suppliers. It is strengthened
with a filler such as plaster of Paris and
is ideal for building up sculpted shapes
that can then be covered with strips of
paper ready for decorating.

Primer

Painting papier mâché shapes with
one or two coats of white acrylic
primer will provide a good surface
for decoration.

Sanding sealer/shellac

This toffee-coloured, spirit-based
lacquer can be used to seal and
strengthen paper and card and to give
an antique look to painted finishes.

Varnish

Several coats of glossy acrylic or
oil-based varnish protect a painted
surface and make colours glow.
Crackle varnish is a two-part
treatment that gives an antique look
and is especially effective with
decoupage designs.

The equipment needed for working with paper and card is minimal, and you will probably already have nearly everything you need. Some woodworking tools are useful when shaping papier mâché.

Paper and Card Equipment

Abrasive paper

Hard papier mâché can be smoothed by rubbing it down with medium- and fine-grade abrasive paper.

Blender

If you want to make your own papier mâché pulp, whizzing the soaked and boiled paper in a blender produces a smooth texture very easily.

Bowl

Use an old mixing bowl to dilute PVA (white) glue or mix wallpaper paste for papier mâché.

Craft (utility) knife

Replace the blade of a craft knife or scalpel often as paper and card will quickly blunt it. Always use a cutting mat to protect the work surface.

Cutting mat

A self-healing cutting mat is an ideal cutting surface.

Paintbrushes

A selection of artist's brushes is useful for applying glue and smoothing down layers of papier mâché as well as for painting. To paint decorative lines use a coachliner (liner) brush: this has long hairs of uniform length and is designed to hold a lot of paint so that you don't have to keep lifting the brush to reload it.

Pencil and ruler

For tracing templates and marking out designs. Use a metal ruler with a craft knife to cut straight lines.

Scissors

Use general household scissors for cutting paper and card. Don't use dressmaking shears as they will quickly be blunted. A pair of small, sharp-pointed scissors is essential for cutting out decoupage images accurately.

Sponge

A natural sponge can be used to create paint effects, to stick down decoupage motifs and wipe off excess paste, and to apply glazes.

Many different decorative techniques are possible using paper and card: just experiment with the materials that inspire you. Papier mâché and papier mâché pulp are both excellent for sculpting items of jewellery.

Paper and Card Techniques

Papier Mâché

Newspaper is most commonly used for papier mâché and is very pliable and strong. For very delicate items you could try using tissue paper, though it is tricky to handle when wet.

1 Tear the newspaper into strips about 2cm/³⁄₄in wide. Tearing with the grain makes it easy to produce regular strips. Dilute PVA (white) glue with water to the consistency of single (light) cream or use fungicide-free wallpaper paste.

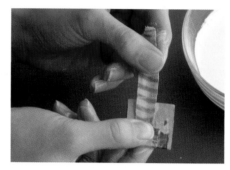

2 Use a paintbrush to coat each strip of paper in the glue or paste and press it on to a cardboard base, or into a mould. Use the brush to smooth the paper down and expel any air bubbles.

3 When you have built up the shape, leave to dry completely. Sand the surface smooth if necessary and hide the newsprint with two coats of white acrylic primer before decorating.

Making Papier Mâché Pulp

Prepared pulp can be bought but it's easy to make. You will need:

5 sheets newspaper
60ml/4 tbsp PVA (white) glue
10ml/2 tsp plaster of Paris
10ml/2 tsp linseed oil

Tear the paper into small squares, place in an old saucepan with water to cover and simmer for 30 minutes. Pour into a blender and blend to a pulp. Add the other ingredients and stir vigorously. Pulp can be stored for some weeks in a plastic box.

Working with Papier Mâché Pulp

You can use paper pulp very effectively to build up sculpted forms, simply pushing it into shape with your fingers. Allow plenty of time for the pulp to dry out thoroughly before completing the project.

1 To make a three-dimensional piece, build up the papier mâché pulp on a base such as a cardboard shape. Leave to dry out thoroughly.

2 When the pulp shape is dry and hard, cover it completely with two layers of papier mâché and leave to dry before decorating.

Decoupage

Though most often associated with furniture and decorative household items, paper cutouts can be used to enhance many different objects, large or small. Glass, metal, wood and china are all suitable surfaces.

Surface Preparation

Whatever you are decorating, it is vital to have an absolutely smooth surface to achieve a "painted on" look.

1 Sand wood smooth with medium- then fine-grade abrasive paper. Prime and sand again, then apply two coats of paint. If you want to leave the wood grain visible, seal the surface with shellac before decorating.

2 Metal should be scrubbed and coated with red oxide primer to provide a key for paint. If you are using a light-coloured paint, apply one or two coats of white acrylic primer.

Painting Edges

On items such as boxes, painted edges can enhance a decoupage design. Choose a colour that contrasts with the base colour and goes well with the cutout designs. It's advisable to paint lines before adding cutouts, in case of mistakes.

Load a coachliner (liner) brush with acrylic paint diluted with a little water. Holding the brush like a pen, and using the edge of your hand as a support, drag the brush towards you. Use your little finger against the edge to keep your hand steady. Lift the brush gradually when you get near the end of the line so that it doesn't drag over the edge. If you need to reload the brush before reaching the end, overlap the lines a little to ensure continuity.

Tinting Prints

Black and white prints are easily enhanced with delicate colour.

Subtle effects can be achieved using coloured pencils. Start with the lighter areas, working with gentle strokes in one direction. Build up the colour gradually, blending it carefully. Seal tinted prints with sanding sealer and leave to dry before cutting out.

Cutting Out Motifs

Whether you prefer to use a pair of scissors or a craft (utility) knife, the basic principles remain the same. Always use a cutting mat with a craft knife.

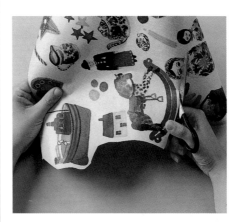

1 Cut the excess paper from around the outer edge of the motif using a large pair of scissors.

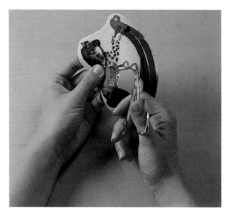

2 Cut away any background areas within the design, piercing a hole in the centre of the area then cutting outwards to the edge. Cut around the outside edge without leaving any trace of background: it is better to cut slightly inside the edge of the motif.

Gluing Motifs

PVA (white) glue is suitable for decoupage on most surfaces. Dilute the glue with a little water to make it spreadable. A glue stick can be used for very small designs, especially on paper or card (stock).

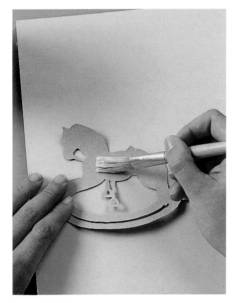

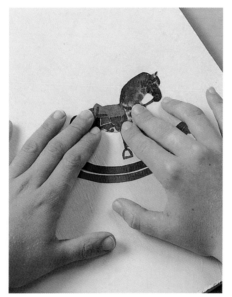

1 Use an artist's brush to paint glue over the back of the motif, thinly covering the entire surface right up to the edges. Alternatively, if the motif has a very intricate design and might be damaged by the brush, you can paint the glue on the base surface, wiping away any excess while still wet after positioning the motif.

2 Lay the cutout gently on the surface. When you are satisfied with its position, press it down gently with your fingers or a barely moistened sponge, starting at the centre and smoothing outwards. When you are working on a small piece you can hold the work up to the light to highlight any air bubbles or areas that have not adhered properly.

3 Lift any edges that have been missed and dab on some more glue if necessary. Leave for a few minutes then gently wipe away excess glue using a damp sponge and leave to dry.

Varnishing

Careful varnishing protects the decoupage, adds depth to the design and completes the illusion that it is a painted surface. Build the varnish up in a series of thin coats, sanding gently between each. Matt (flat) acrylic varnish is easy to apply and dries quickly, but you may like to finish with a few coats of durable oil-based varnish to protect the surface. For an aged effect brush a little thinned raw umber paint over the varnished surface, leave a few minutes, then wipe off with a cloth.

◀ A crackle finish gives an antique look. It can be applied over varnish and consists of two layers: a slow-drying base and a quick-drying top coat that cracks as the first layer dries out. Apply the second coat when the first feels dry but slightly tacky. If no cracks appear as it dries the process can be speeded up by playing a cool hairdryer over the surface. Rub a little artist's oil paint into the cracks to emphasize them: raw umber is the colour most commonly used. Finish with two coats of oil-based varnish.

Wood is an infinitely adaptable material to work with. Chunky wooden beads and bangles make the most of its natural grain and colours, but it's also an ideal base for paint and other applied decorations.

Woodworking Materials and Equipment

Abrasive paper
Small abrasive particles, glued to backing paper, are graded according to their size: the finer the grit, the smoother the finish.

Bradawl/Awl
The sharp point can be twisted into wood without splitting the grain and is used for scribing and piercing guide holes for drilling.

Drill
A hand drill can be used for quickly making small holes in wood to take jewellery fixings. An electric mini-drill is a convenient alternative.

Glue
PVA (white) glue dries clear and is ideal for joining pieces of wood, though for small projects a hot glue gun is fast and convenient. Use strong epoxy resin glue to attach jewellery findings securely.

Paintbrushes
You could use artist's brushes for most jobs, but ideally use a fine decorating brush for primers and undercoats and artist's brushes to decorate small pieces. Varnishing brushes have long, flat bristles to minimize brush marks.

Paints
Acrylic paints are ideal for painting wood. Start with a coat or two of white acrylic primer to give a smooth, clean surface so that the colours of your design look clear and bright.

Plywood
Birch-faced plywood is smooth and strong and because of its construction will not warp or split. Thin plywood suitable for small projects such as badges is available in small sheets from model and craft suppliers.

Saws
Frame saws are designed for intricate cutting. They work on the pull stroke so blades should always be fitted with the points facing towards the handle.
Coping saw – This is fine for small projects and can be fitted with a range of disposable blades.
Fretsaw – This cuts more deeply than the coping saw as it has a larger frame.

Square
A try square is essential for accurate marking out of right angles.

Varnish
Both acrylic and oil-based varnishes are available in a range of finishes from matt to high gloss. Several thin coats of gloss varnish will make bright paint colours glow like enamels.

Fine details are all-important when you are working on a small scale. Accurate marking out and cutting, meticulous smoothing of the wood, and painstaking surface finishes are the keys to success.

Woodworking Techniques

Transferring Designs

◀ **1** Draw or trace the design and scale it up if necessary by copying it on graph paper of a larger scale or using the enlarging facility on a photocopier. Cut out an accurate template from thin card (stock) and draw around it on the wood using a sharp pencil. For square or rectangular items such as boxes it's essential to check all right angles with a try square when marking out the component parts.

2 Use compasses to draw circles directly on wood. For a motif such as a sun, adjust the compasses and draw an inner circle as a guide for drawing the rays.

Using a Frame Saw

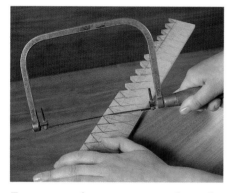

Fret saws and coping saws work on the pull stroke for accurate control. The frame allows the blade to be swivelled for cutting curves. The wood should be clamped so that there is clearance underneath all the lines of the design to move the saw.

If you are cutting out a pierced design, use a hand drill to make a starter hole in each inner section. The removable blade of the saw can then be fed through and re-attached. Saw carefully to the edge of the marked shape and then follow the outline.

Smoothing Surfaces

Many different materials are used to make abrasive papers, generally known as sandpapers. Glasspaper, in medium and fine grades, is suitable for smoothing wood before decorating. Silicon carbide paper is more hardwearing. Dark grey silicon paper, known as "wet and dry" paper, needs lubricating with water and can be used for fine smoothing of painted and varnished finishes on wood.

Sand all sawn edges until they feel smooth and splinter-free to the touch. Wrap a square of abrasive paper around a wooden or cork sanding block for best results on flat surfaces. Make sure the block is free of defects to avoid scoring the surface of the wood.

For smoothing curved areas wrap a small piece of abrasive paper around your finger, or fold it abrasive side out to get into tight angles.

This glittering star-shaped brooch in papier mâché makes an ideal birthday badge if you decorate it with the appropriate sign of the zodiac: the colourful design used here represents Cancer the Crab.

Star-sign Brooch

you will need

scrap paper, pencil and scissors (for template)

corrugated cardboard

craft (utility) knife

self-healing cutting mat

newspaper

PVA (white) glue

artist's brushes

white acrylic primer

gouache paints: light blue, yellow, red

gloss acrylic varnish

gold enamel paint

brooch back

epoxy resin glue

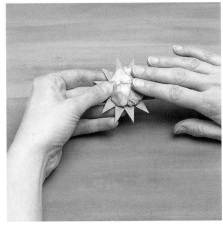

1 Draw a star shape on to scrap paper, cut it out and draw around this shape on to the corrugated cardboard. Now cut out the cardboard star shape. Soak some newspaper in diluted PVA glue, scrunch it up and mound it in the centre of the star.

2 Cover the whole brooch in several layers of newspaper strips soaked in PVA glue. Allow to dry.

3 Give the brooch a coat of PVA glue, then one of white acrylic primer. Allow to dry, paint on the design and then the clear gloss varnish.

4 Add gold enamel paint details. Finally, fix a brooch back in place using epoxy resin glue.

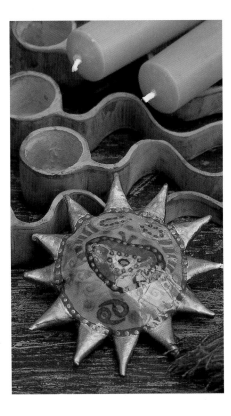

Use papier mâché to create an unusual summery bracelet, decorated with slices of different citrus fruits. Glints of gold picking out the details on the fruit echo the sparkling gold foil lining inside.

Fruity Bracelet

you will need

tracing paper, pencil, paper or card
(stock) (for template)

scissors

thin cardboard

masking tape

large hook and eye

newspaper

PVA (white) glue

strong clear glue

artist's brushes

gold foil (from a chocolate wrapper)

white acrylic primer

acrylic paints: yellow, red,
orange and gold

gloss acrylic varnish

1 Copy the template at the back of the book, enlarging it to fit your wrist, to make a paper or card template. Use this template to cut the shape out of thin cardboard. Tape a large hook to one end of the cardboard bracelet and a matching eye to the other.

2 Tear newspaper into strips and soak in diluted PVA glue. Cover the cardboard with several layers of papier mâché, covering all the edges neatly. Leave to dry. Use strong, clear glue to stick a sheet of gold foil to the inside of the bracelet. Trim the edges.

3 Prime the outside of the bracelet with a coat of white acrylic primer to smooth the surface. Decorate with slices of citrus fruit using acrylic paints. Add touches of gold paint around the edges, pips and dimples.

4 When the paint is dry, protect with several coats of gloss acrylic varnish.

Beads made from paper were traditionally used to make bead curtains, but this old technique can also transform good-quality printed paper into colourful abstract designs for beautiful necklaces and bracelets.

Rolled-paper Beads

you will need
ruler
pencil
gift wrap
scissors
glue stick or PVA (white) glue
gloss acrylic varnish
varnish brush
thin elastic

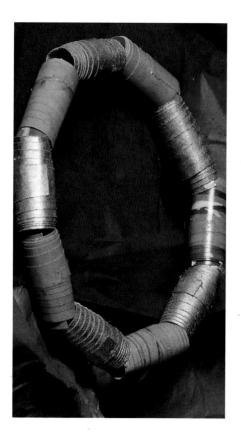

1 Draw a series of 2.5cm/1in-wide strips on the back of a sheet of gift wrap. Now make a mark halfway along one short edge of each strip. Draw lines from the two opposite corners to the marked point, in such a way that you are dividing the strip into long, thin triangles.

2 Cut along the lines on each strip. The central triangle will make a symmetrical bead. Use the right-angled triangles if you want to make conical beads, such as for earrings or the ends of a necklace.

3 Starting at the base of the triangle, roll each strip of paper tightly around a pencil. Make sure the end is correctly aligned with the pencil when you begin so that the bead is symmetrical. After the first turn, apply glue to the wrong side of the paper.

4 Put a little extra glue on the end of the paper triangle and press it down firmly. Leave the bead on the pencil until the glue is dry. The beads can be strengthened and protected with a few coats of acrylic varnish before they are threaded on thin elastic.

This exotic piece of jewellery is made from papier mâché pulp, hand-painted in gorgeous colours and then decorated with artificial gemstones and glass tear-drops.

Winged Cupid Brooch

you will need

tracing paper

pencil

thin card (stock)

craft (utility) knife

cutting mat

papier mâché pulp

newspaper

PVA (white) glue

white acrylic primer

artist's brushes

flat-backed glass gems

epoxy resin glue

dressmaker's pin

eye-hook pins

gouache paints

matt (flat) acrylic varnish

gold enamel paint

small glass tear-drop beads

small jump-rings

round-nosed (snub-nosed) pliers

brooch back

1 Trace the template from the back of the book, transfer it to card and cut out all of the sections. Cover the card pieces with papier mâché pulp and apply several layers of newspaper strips soaked in PVA glue. Allow to dry completely.

2 Paint with a coat of PVA glue, then with white primer. Glue on the glass gems using epoxy resin glue. Make holes using a pin and insert the eye-hook pins, securing them with epoxy resin glue.

3 Paint on the design with gouache paints. When dry, coat with matt varnish. Leave to dry again, then add gold enamel details.

4 Assemble all the brooch pieces and tear-drop beads, joining them with jump-rings (using the pliers). Glue the brooch back into position.

This little trinket box with its pretty posy of roses is ideal for small pieces of jewellery and adds a feminine touch to a dressing-table. Crackle varnish gives the rose design a lovely antique look.

Decoupage Roses Box

1 Remove the box lid. Paint the box with a coat of acrylic primer and leave to dry. Lightly sand the surface, then follow with two coats of cream emulsion paint.

2 Now prepare some antique-effect gold paint by mixing a little raw umber and artist's gold acrylic paint with just a touch of water. Then, very carefully lay your coachliner brush in the gold paint and ensure that the brush is thoroughly covered.

▲ **3** Place the brush on one edge of the box rim and drag it along to the end. Now paint all of the edges on the base and lid of your box with gold paint, as described in step 2. Leave until completely dry. Follow with an even coat of acrylic varnish, used to protect the base colour.

▲ **4** With small sharp-pointed scissors, cut out the rose-heads, making sure that you choose colours that complement each other. Use different designs for the front and sides.

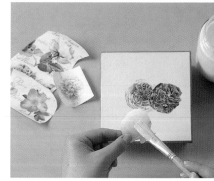

▲ **5** Measure the width and length of the box lid with a ruler to find the centre. Mark this point with a pencil. Dilute some PVA glue with a little water and brush it on to the back of the first rose. Stick it in the centre of the box lid, then add the rest, one at a time, around the central rose until you have a circle.

6 Fit the lid on to the base but don't screw the hinges back on. Apply the designs to the back, front and sides, sticking your motifs over the join (seam) of the lid and base. Leave the box to dry.

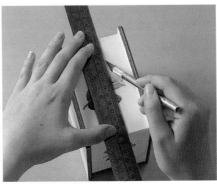

◀ **7** Place a metal ruler along the edge of the join over which you have stuck the motif and draw a very sharp craft knife along the join, making sure that you cut really cleanly through the paper. Repeat on the other two sides.

▶

8 Seal the the surface by brushing on 5–10 coats of acrylic varnish. Allow each coat to dry throughly before applying the next.

9 Following the manufacturer's instructions, brush on the first stage of the crackle varnish and leave until slightly tacky to the touch (about 1–2 hours, although this can vary).

10 Brush on the second stage of the crackle varnish, making sure that you have covered all areas. Leave to dry naturally for about 1–2 hours.

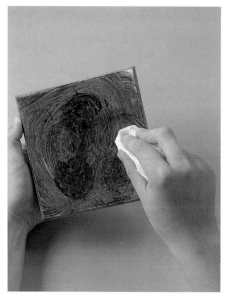

11 If no cracks have appeared, use a hairdryer on its lowest setting and move it over the surface until the cracks begin to appear.

12 Put a tiny amount of raw umber oil paint on to kitchen paper moistened with white spirit and wipe over all surfaces of the box.

13 Take a clean sheet of kitchen paper and wipe off the excess, leaving the paint only in the cracks. Leave to dry overnight. Varnish with two coats of oil-based varnish. Screw the lid and base of the box back together.

Wear one of these jolly badges as a colourful and bold brooch on a plain coat or sweater. Simple to make, these badges are bound to lift your spirits in the morning.

Sun and Moon Badges

you will need

tracing paper, pencil, card (stock) and scissors (for templates)

5mm/¼in birch plywood sheet

coping saw or fretsaw

medium- and fine-grade abrasive paper

white acrylic primer

artist's brushes

acrylic paints: yellow, red and blue

gloss acrylic varnish

epoxy resin or hot glue

2 brooch backs

1 Make card templates (size as wished) from those at the back of the book, and draw round them on to the wood. Cut out the shapes with the saw and sand the edges smooth.

2 Paint both sides and all the edges of the shapes with white acrylic primer. When the paint is dry, sand the surfaces lightly until smooth.

3 Paint the fronts of the sun and moon with acrylic paint and add the features and other details. When the paint is dry, add a coat of varnish and leave to dry. Put a thick line of glue on the back of each badge and press the brooch back firmly into the glue.

The sunflower is an enduringly popular image and an effective stylized motif. Simply painted in warm yellows, this cheerful little badge makes a bright decoration for a plain sweater or a denim jacket.

Sunflower Badge

you will need

5mm/¼in birch plywood sheet
pencil
pair of compasses
coping saw or fretsaw
medium- and fine-grade
abrasive paper
PVA (white) glue
white acrylic primer
artist's brushes
acrylic paints: yellow, red,
chocolate-brown and gold
gloss acrylic varnish
brooch back
epoxy resin glue

1 Draw a circle for the flower-centre on the plywood with the compasses. Draw the petals freehand around the centre. Draw another circle the same size as the centre. Cut out these two shapes with a saw.

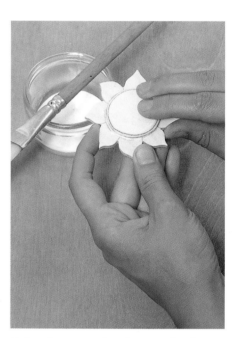

2 Sand any rough edges on the flower and sand the edge of the circle to a curve. Glue the circle to the centre of the flower shape using PVA glue. Paint with white primer and allow to dry. Sand lightly.

◄ **3** Paint in the flower details with the acrylic paints. Mix yellow and red to make a golden-yellow for the petals. Paint the centre brown. When dry, add gold dots to the centre. Apply a coat of gloss varnish. Attach the brooch back using epoxy resin glue.

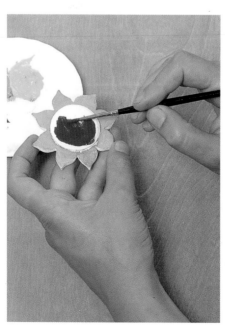

This jolly little shooting star can be decorated as fancifully as you like in brilliant contrasting colours. Use pearlized paint for its tail and add several coats of glossy varnish to make the colours glow.

Shooting Star Badge

you will need

tracing paper

pencil

4mm/⅙in birch plywood sheet

coping saw or fretsaw

medium- and fine-grade abrasive paper

white acrylic primer

artist's brushes

acrylic paints

water-based pearlized paints

gloss acrylic varnish

brooch back

epoxy resin glue

1 Trace the template at the back of the book and transfer to the plywood. Cut out. Sand all the edges.

2 Paint with a coat of white acrylic primer. When dry, sand lightly and mark the remaining points of the star.

3 Paint on the badge's design in acrylic paints, using pearlized paint for the tail. Protect with several coats of gloss varnish.

4 Glue the brooch back on to the badge using epoxy resin glue.

This attractive little box is easy to construct, but the delicate painting and the raised crab design make it unusual and eye-catching. The lid is decorated with a wavy pattern inspired by the crab's watery home.

Crab Jewel Box

you will need

coping saw or fretsaw

40cm/16in pine slat, 3cm x 8mm/ 1¼ x ⅜in

4mm/⅙in birch plywood sheet

ruler

tracing paper, pencil, card (stock) and scissors (for template)

abrasive paper

wood glue

masking tape

artist's brushes

white acrylic primer

acrylic paints: blue, gold and red

matt (flat) acrylic varnish

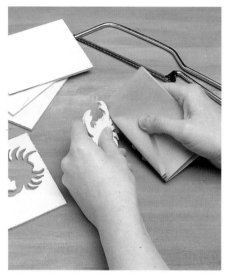

1 Cut the pine slat into four 10cm/4in lengths. From the plywood cut two rectangles measuring 8 x 10cm/3¼ x 4in for the base and lid insert, and one measuring 11.5 x 10cm/4½ x 4in for the lid. Enlarge the crab template at the back of the book, transfer it to the plywood and cut it out. Remove rough edges with abrasive paper.

2 Assemble the sides of the box and stick with wood glue. Hold the sides in place with masking tape until the glue is completely dry. Glue in the base. Glue the lid insert centrally on to the lid. Sand again to smooth any rough edges.

◀ **3** Paint the box and crab with a coat of white acrylic primer. Sand lightly when dry. Paint the box and the lid in blue, thinned with water and applied with wavy brushstrokes. Paint on the border pattern and stars. Paint the crab in red and pick out details in blue and gold. Finish off with a coat of varnish. When dry, glue the crab firmly on to the lid of the box.

Clay and Glass

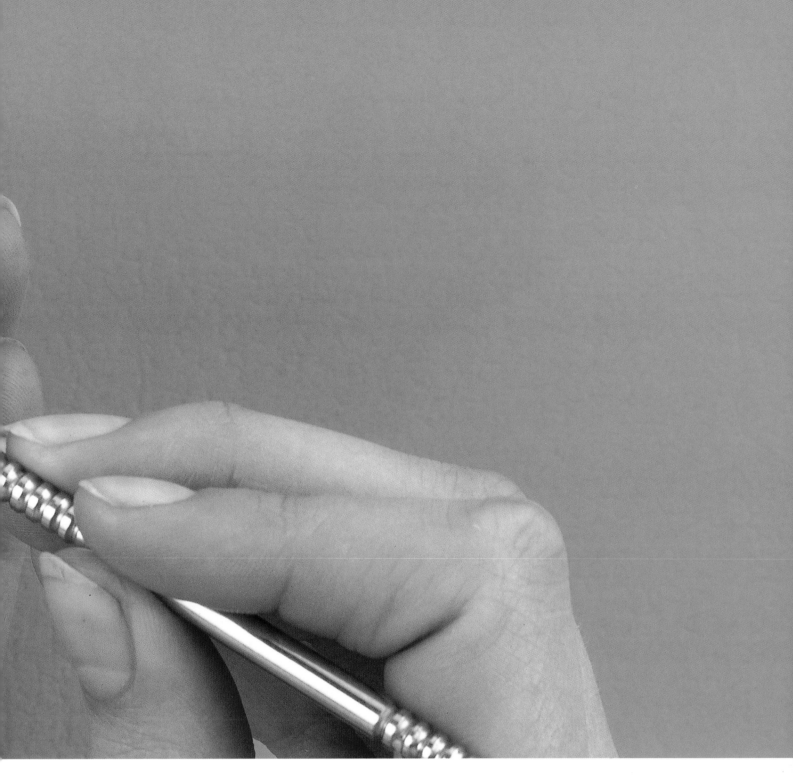

Modelling clay is an ideal medium for intricate ornaments such as buttons, earrings and beads. You can roll it, coil it and shape it in fancy moulds, and a host of different surface textures are possible. Using polymer clay, which is made in a huge range of colours and special effects, you can even achieve complex millefiori designs and sophisticated metallic finishes. The chapter ends with a sparkling idea for a pretty glass trinket box.

Choose from self-hardening modelling clay – which does not require firing and can be painted, varnished or gilded once dry – or colourful polymer clay, which is hardened by baking in a domestic oven.

Claywork Materials

Bronze powder

This is a fine metallic powder that is available in gold, silver, copper and other colours. Mix the powder with varnish and brush on to produce a gilded effect.

Button backs

Self-cover buttons are useful for making clay buttons.

Clay hardeners

Powdered hardeners can be mixed into modelling clay before the clay is shaped and they harden the clay throughout. Liquid hardeners seal and harden the outside only.

Glass gemstones and beads

Beads for embedding in clay should be flat-backed. If beads are mounted in clay that is to be fired, they must be made of glass.

Glue

PVA (white) glue will be suitable for holding hardened clay, but epoxy resin is stronger. Diluted PVA glue is commonly used as a sealant on modelling clay.

Jewellery wire

Use this fine wire to connect clay pieces for jewellery items such as earrings and necklaces.

Metallic leaf

Both modelling clay and polymer clay can be gilded. Dutch metal leaf, in gold, silver, copper and aluminium, is easier to apply than real gold.

Modelling clay

Clay comes in many brands and qualities. Air-dried modelling clay needs no firing, but you can strengthen some brands by baking or adding hardeners. Follow manufacturer's instructions.

Paint

Artist's acrylics or acrylic craft paints are suitable for decorating modelling clay and can also be applied to polymer clay. Many effects are possible with special paints: metallic or pearlized colour, verdigris and crackle glaze.

Polymer clay

Actually a plastic (polyvinyl chloride), polymer clay is clean to work with, does not shrink and needs only a low-temperature firing. Already coloured, it needs no further decoration except for special effects such as gilding. It is available in many colours, plus translucent and glow-in-the-dark effects.

Varnish

Gloss or matt (flat) varnish specially formulated for polymer clay is available. Acrylic spray varnish is convenient for small projects.

The most important tools required for working with modelling and polymer clay are your hands. Many ordinary items such as knitting needles, dough cutters and knives can be used for shaping clay.

Claywork Equipment

Airtight boxes and bags

Polymer clay goes crumbly if exposed to heat and daylight. Wrap it in greaseproof paper before storing it in a box. Spare modelling clay should be kept soft inside a plastic bag – moisten the inside of the bag if necessary.

Baking parchment

A sheet of parchment taped to the work surface gives a smooth surface for modelling. Finished models can also be placed on it for baking.

Brayer

This small roller is used to smooth clay and for applying metal leaf.

Knives

A very sharp slim-bladed craft (utility) knife is needed when working with small pieces of polymer clay, and a surgical tissue blade can cut very thin slices without distorting patterns.

Mirror

Placed behind the work, a mirror helps you to see all round the clay for accurate cutting and shaping.

Modelling tools

Many different shapes are available for shaping and smoothing clay. Dental probes make excellent precision tools for modelling. Cocktail sticks and toothpicks are often useful.

Oven

Polymer clay can be hardened in a domestic oven. Accurate temperature control is important as clay burns easily but is fragile if undercooked.

Paintbrushes

Artist's brushes are needed for applying paints and bronze powders.

Pasta machine

Use this to roll out polymer clay to precise, even thicknesses and to mix colours together. Keep a machine solely for use with clay, and wipe it clean when changing colours.

Pastry cutters and moulds

Cake decorating suppliers are a good source of tools. A wheeled pastry cutter can be used to make zigzag edges. Skewers are useful for shaping clay and for holding clay beads during baking.

Perspex (Plexiglas)

This rigid clear plastic makes a smooth modelling surface and a small sheet is used to roll polymer clay canes to reduce their diameter uniformly.

Rolling pin

A vinyl or straight-sided glass roller is best for rolling out clay.

As polymer clay picks up any dirt and dust around, your hands must be scrupulously clean and you should wash them each time you change from one colour to another, to avoid discolouring the clay.

Polymer Clay Techniques

Preparing Polymer Clay

The clay must be kneaded before it is worked. As it is responsive to temperature the warmth of your hands contributes to the conditioning process. Work small amounts, about one-eighth of a block, at a time. Roll the clay into a sausage between your palms then bend it over and roll again, until it is soft and pliable. Try to avoid trapping air bubbles. A pasta machine can be used to knead the clay and to mix colours.

Mixing Colours

Although polymer clay is available in many colours, you can mix more subtle shades yourself. When mixing dark and light colours add tiny bits of the dark clay to the lighter colour to avoid overpowering it.

Rolling out

A pasta machine can be used to produce sheets of uniform thickness, or you can roll the clay out by hand on a smooth clean surface.

To achieve an even thickness throughout the sheet, place two equal-sized pieces of wood, metal or plastic, matching the required depth, on either side of the clay.

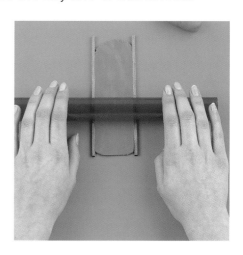

1 Twist together two or more sausages of clay in different colours.

Making Beads

A basic round bead is made by simply rolling a ball of clay between the palms of your hands. You may find that it is quite difficult to make a hole in soft clay without distorting it, so an effective alternative method is to drill the hole after the clay has been baked.

2 Roll the twisted clay into a smooth log then twist, stretch and double over, excluding any air. The clay can be used in this marbled state. Continue to work it to blend colours completely.

1 Make a hole in an unbaked bead using a drilling action with a tapered tool such as a darning needle. When it emerges, remove it and push it through from the other side to neaten the hole.

2 To prevent beads distorting during baking, support them on skewers or wire, suspended across a baking tray.

Clay Cane Work

Clay sheets of different colours can be stacked or rolled together with gentle pressure and then sliced to create a variety of patterns. Derived from glassworking techniques, cane work creates a roll with a design running along its length from which slices can be cut.

Jelly Roll

This technique creates a log that is sliced to create a simple spiral pattern.

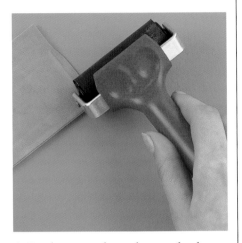

1 Stack two or three sheets of polymer clay together and trim the edges to form a rectangle. Roll a brayer over one of the shorter edges to taper it.

2 Starting at the tapered end, roll up the layers tightly and evenly. Roll the cane to smooth the seam and trim each end flat.

Picture Cane

Simple images can be made into canes. Choose a strong shape and use boldly contrasting colours so that the picture stays clear when the size is reduced.

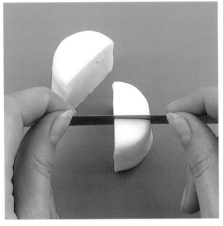

1 Roll a cane of white polymer clay about 3.5cm/1½in in diameter. Cut it in half lengthways using a tissue blade. Curve one half to make the duck's body and cut the other half in two to make two quarters.

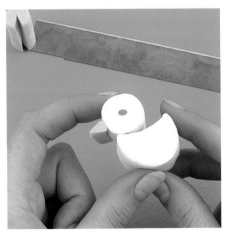

3 Place the head on the body. Cut a triangular wedge from a 1cm/½in diameter yellow cane and press it against the head to form the bill.

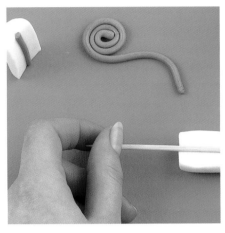

2 Roll one quarter into a round and cut in half again. Make a groove down the middle of one flat side and run a thin sausage of blue clay down it. Groove the other half and sandwich together to make the head and eye.

4 Pack the gaps around the duck with wedges of blue clay to make a circular shape and wrap with a thin sheet to hold it together. Roll to consolidate the pieces and surround with a sheet of dark blue. Roll the cane to smooth the join and trim the concave ends.

Flower Cane

Choose colours that contrast strongly to give the design clarity. Slices are best cut using a tissue blade: chill the cane if necessary to avoid distorting the pattern.

Complex Canes

To reduce canes' size, roll them under a small sheet of Perspex (Plexiglas).

1 Roll one cane for the flower centre, five for the petals and two for the leaves, each about 2cm/¾in wide. Wrap the centre cane in a thin sheet of a contrasting colour, and the petals in a different colour. Roll the canes to smooth the seams.

2 Cut the leaf canes lengthways into quarters. Roll out a thin sheet of a new colour. Arrange the canes to form a flower and wrap the bundle in the prepared sheet. Roll the cane to compact it, and trim the ends.

To make canes of different diameters, stop rolling at each size required and cut the cane in half. Reserve one half and continue to roll the other. Different canes can be joined and rolled together to create complex designs.

Metallic Finishes

Polymer clay can be decorated by brushing on metallic powders, or metal leaf can be applied to a sheet of clay before it is shaped.

1 Lay a sheet of Dutch metal leaf, metal side down, over a sheet of clay. Roll over it with a brayer as you lay it down to exclude air bubbles. Rub all over the backing paper then gently and slowly peel it off.

2 For a crackle finish, cover the applied metal leaf with another piece of paper and roll a brayer over the paper until the required amount of cracking is achieved.

3 Any mould can be used to shape polymer clay or impress a texture in the surface. To gild a moulded piece, lightly brush the mould with metallic powder before embossing the clay.

Provided it is kept damp and soft when not in use, modelling clay is easy to handle and shape. Always keep spare clay covered with plastic wrap or in a plastic bag.

Modelling Clay Techniques

Preparing Clay

Knead the clay until it is soft and malleable and all air bubbles are eliminated. Colour can either be kneaded into the clay before modelling or painted on once the finished model has hardened.

Mixing Clay with Colour

Use a concentrated colouring agent such as paste food colouring, which will produce intense colours without making the clay too wet.

1 Add colour gradually to achieve the shade you want. Remember that the shade will change slightly when the clay dries out.

2 Roll the clay into a long sausage, fold over and repeat. Add more colour as necessary and repeat until the colour is evenly distributed.

Mixing Clay with Hardener

This treatment makes the clay more difficult to work with, so keep it in a plastic bag. You can soften it slightly by kneading in a little hand cream.

1 Make an indentation in the clay and add powder hardener. Fold the clay over the powder and knead a little before rolling into a sausage.

2 Fold the sausage over and add more hardener. Continue to knead until you have used all the powder you need.

Decorating Clay

A wide variety of decorative techniques, such as sponging and gilding, can be used on modelling clay.

Some types of self-hardening clay have a tendency to flake, so it is a good idea to seal the surface with one or two coats of diluted PVA (white) glue.

Apply paint to modelling clay with a brush or sponge, and spray or brush on a minimum of two coats of varnish.

Drying Clay

To avoid cracking, dry clay gradually, covering it with a damp cloth to slow the process.

Tape small, flat clay pieces to a board in order to prevent them from curling, adding a weight if necessary. Remove any rough edges when dry with some fine abrasive paper.

Glass in a variety of colours and textures is available from specialist stained glass suppliers, together with glass paints, self-adhesive foil and other materials, some of which may also be found in craft stores.

Glassworking Materials

Contour paste

This creates raised lines on glass to act as a barrier for glass paints.

Copper foil

Wrap this tape around the edges of glass so panes can be soldered together.

Borax-based flux (auflux)

This is brushed on to clean metal while soldering and to make solder flow well.

Glass

Clear picture glass can be used to make small boxes and panels. Stained glass is made in many colours and different effects. Small pieces of mirror add extra sparkle.

Glass nuggets

Widely available in many different colours and sizes, glass nuggets can be glued on to decorate glass and other surfaces. They combine effectively with glass paints.

Glue

Two-part epoxy resin glue takes a few minutes to harden, which gives you some time to position the elements of a piece. Ultra-violet glue hardens in daylight, but is not suitable for gluing red glass as the colour blocks ultra-violet rays.

Solder

Various different formulations of metal alloys are currently manufactured for use as solder. When working with glass, solder is used to join panels framed in copper foil, and 50:50 tin and lead is best for this purpose, as it flows easily.

Wire

Copper wire is ideal for use with foiled glass panes as it is compatible with tin solder. It can be used for making loops and hooks, or for decoration. Silver jewellery wire can be used as a decorative binding.

Working with glass does require some specialist equipment, all of which can be purchased from glass suppliers. You will probably already have many of the other items you need.

Glassworking Equipment

Craft (utility) knife
A craft knife will cut through lead and copper foil.

Fid
This tapered wooden tool is used for pressing down copper foil and self-adhesive lead.

Flux brush
This is used to paint borax-based flux (auflux) on to copper foil.

Glass cutter
A glass cutter has a hardened metal wheel that is run over the glass to score it. The glass can then be broken along the scored line.

Gloves
Wear gloves to protect your hands from glass splinters and toxic lead.

Goggles
It is always essential to wear goggles when working with glass.

Lint-free cloth
Use clean, dry rags to polish glass.

Pliers
Grozing pliers are used to take off any sharp shards of glass. Round-nosed (snub-nosed) and square-nosed pliers are useful for straightening and curling wire and bending sharp angles.

Scythe stone
Otherwise known as a glass file, a cigar-shaped scythe stone is used to file down the sharp or jagged edges left after glass has been cut. Use this tool on every piece of glass you cut before doing any further work on it.

Soldering iron
You will need a 75-watt (or higher) soldering iron, and a stand to support it when it is hot.

Wire cutters
Use these to cut wire neatly.

Practise scoring and cutting spare pieces of plain picture glass before you try it on more expensive stained or etched glass. Always smooth all the cut edges and dispose of waste glass with care.

Glassworking Techniques

Cutting Glass Once the glass has been scored, there are various different ways of breaking it along the line. Try each of the methods illustrated below to see which one works best for you.

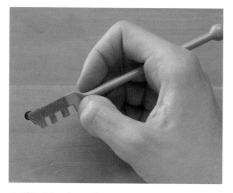

1 Hold the glass cutter with your index finger on top and your thumb and second finger gripping each side, with the grozing teeth facing towards your elbow. When you are cutting correctly, with the cutter at right angles to the glass, this position will give you a lot of movement in your arm.

2 Always cut glass from edge to edge, one cut at a time. Start with the cutter at right angles to the glass and draw it with a consistent pressure from one edge to the other.

3 Now you can break it along the scored line. The first method is to hold the cutter upside down between thumb and first finger, holding it loosely so that you can swing it to hit the underside of the line with the ball on the end. Tap along the line following the crack. The glass will break off.

4 The second method is to hold the glass with your hands on each side of one end of the scored line. Apply firm pressure, pulling down and away from the crack. This works only if the score mark is very straight.

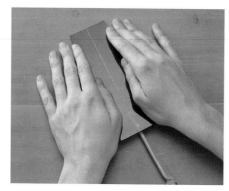

5 The third method is to lay the cutter on the work surface and place the glass on top with the scored line over the cutter.

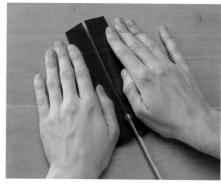

6 Put pressure on both sides of the line with the bases of your thumbs. Push down until the glass breaks.

Foiling Glass Self-adhesive copper foil has a protective backing paper which you should remove just as you are applying the foil to the glass. Try not to touch the adhesive as any grease or dust will stop it sticking.

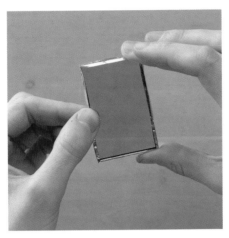

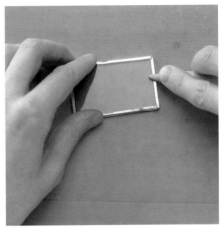

1 With the piece of glass in one hand, hold the foil between the fingers of your other hand and use your thumb to peel back the backing paper as you work around the edges of the glass.

2 Stick the foil to the edges of the glass all the way around, and overlap the ends by 1cm/½in.

3 Using two fingertips, press the foil down on to both sides of the glass all the way around. Use a fid to flatten the foil on to the glass to make sure it is firmly stuck.

Soldering Glass Foiling the edges of glass panes allows you to join them by soldering the metal. It's a good idea to tack together all the elements of a design with a blob of solder on each joint so that you can make any adjustments before completing the soldering.

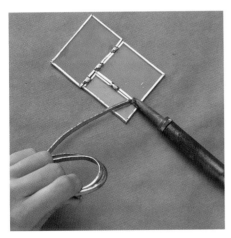

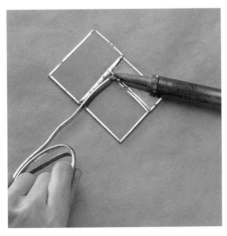

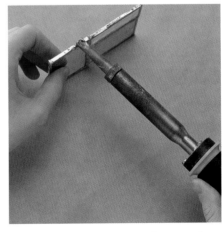

1 Apply flux to all the copper foil showing on the first side. With the hot soldering iron in one hand and the solder in the other, with about 10cm/4in uncoiled, tack the pieces together by melting a blob of solder on to each adjoining edge.

2 To complete the joint, melt the solder and allow it to run along the copper. Do not let it go too flat but aim to build up an evenly rounded seam, which is stronger and looks neater. Turn the piece over and flux and solder the other side of the joint.

3 Tin the edges by first fluxing, then running the soldering iron along each edge. There is usually already enough solder on the edge to spread around.

An easy-to-make clay mould is used to model these eye-catching silver earrings, so it's easy to produce as many pairs as you want – you can make them as gifts for everyone who admires them on you!

Moulded Star Earrings

you will need

self-hardening modelling clay

rolling pin

tracing paper, pencil, paper or thin card (stock) and scissors (for template)

modelling tools

pair of earring studs

bonding adhesive

black acrylic paint

paintbrushes

silver powder

varnish

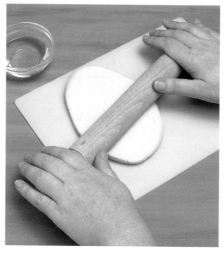

1 Roll out a small piece of clay to a thickness of 8mm/⅜in.

2 Trace the template from the back of the book on to thin card or paper. Cut the star shape out of the clay.

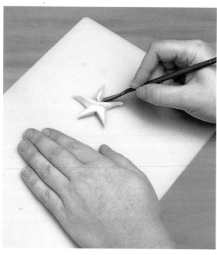

3 Mark a line from the centre of the star to each point where two rays meet and use the flat side of the modelling tool to mould each point to a 90° angle. Smooth the star with water, tuck the edges in neatly and leave to dry.

4 Take a small ball of clay and press with your palm until it is about 2cm/¾in thick. Press in the hardened clay star then lift out carefully without distorting the mould. Leave to dry.

5 Use the mould to make further clay stars. Lift them out of the mould and place face up on the work surface. Trim off the excess clay with a modelling tool. Allow to harden.

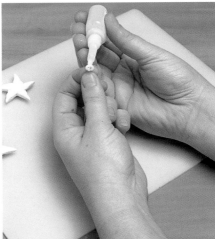

6 Glue an earring stud to the back of each star.

7 Paint the stars with black acrylic paint and leave to dry completely.

8 Mix silver powder with varnish and brush this over the stars to complete.

Brighten up a child's coat (or your own) with these friendly spiders. Use self-cover buttons, matching the size to your buttonholes, and snap the fronts on to the backs before you start to decorate them.

Spider Buttons

you will need
polymer clay: bright green, black and white
self-cover metal buttons
rolling pin
craft (utility) knife
self-healing cutting mat
gloss acrylic varnish
paintbrush

1 Roll the green clay out thinly and cut out a circle large enough to cover one of the buttons. Mould the clay over the button.

2 Using black clay, roll very thin strands for the legs and press them on to the button. Roll a finer strand for the spider's thread.

3 Roll a pea-sized ball of black clay and press it into the centre of the button for the spider's body.

4 Create eyes from two balls of white clay and two tiny balls of black clay. Bake in a low oven following the clay manufacturer's instructions. Apply two coats of gloss varnish when cool.

These very striking earrings shimmer with a distressed black and gold paint effect that looks stunning but is actually quite simple to achieve. The faces are easily modelled out of clay.

Sun and Moon Earrings

you will need
modelling clay
rolling pin
jar lid
modelling tools
earring posts and butterfly backs
strong clear glue
fine-grade abrasive paper
black acrylic paint
artist's brushes
gold powder
matt (flat) acrylic varnish

1 Roll out two pieces of clay, each to a circle about 5mm/¼in thick and 7.5cm/3in in diameter. Use a jar lid as a template to mark an inner circle. With a modelling tool, build up the central area so it is higher than the outer area but still flat.

2 Model the features of your sun on the raised central area with a modelling tool. Mark the rays around the face and cut away the excess clay. Pierce some dots in the face and rays and leave to dry for 1–2 days. Model a moon in the same way.

3 Glue the earring posts in position. Sand between the rays for a smoother look. Paint black. Mix the gold powder with the varnish, then paint. With a semi-dry brush, go over the face up and down quickly, so that the black underneath shows through and accentuates the features of the face. Paint the moon in the same way.

Formalized leaves and gilded scroll-work turn simple square boxes into encrusted Renaissance-style treasures. You could line the inside of each little box with sumptuous fabric to hold small pieces of jewellery.

Florentine Boxes

you will need

square and rectangular cardboard craft boxes

tracing paper

hard and soft pencils

masking tape

modelling clay

modelling tools

PVA (white) glue

medium and fine artist's brushes

acrylic craft paints: white, pale lilac and pale blue

dark and pale gold metallic paint

matt (flat) acrylic spray varnish

1 Enlarge the templates provided to fit the top and sides of the box lid. Trace the outline with a hard pencil, then rub over the reverse with a soft pencil. Tape the paper to the lid. Draw over the lines again using a hard pencil to transfer the design.

2 Make the four leaf shapes from small rolls of modelling clay and press them into position on the box lid. Use modelling tools to add the details, and smooth the clay with a damp finger.

3 Make the dots from small balls of clay. Press them in place with the point of a pencil.

4 Finish the design on top of the lid by adding the four trefoil motifs on the corners.

5 Make the scrolls and leaves for each side of the lid. Allow the clay to dry thoroughly. ▶

6 Paint the lid with PVA glue diluted with an equal quantity of water. When the glue is dry, paint the lid and box with white acrylic paint.

7 Now paint the lid of your box with a base coat of pale lilac.

8 Add a stippling of pale blue paint, applied with an almost dry brush.

9 Using a fine brush, paint the motifs in dark gold. When dry, add pale gold highlights as desired.

10 Give a textured look to the lid by brushing lightly over the surface with a dry brush loaded with a small amount of gold paint.

11 Paint the bottom of the box to match, adding a small amount of gold paint to each edge. Finish with a protective coat of matt varnish.

These jolly earrings, made using the cane technique, will suit the mood of a hot summer's day or cheer up a dull one. Have fun making the orange slices as realistic as you can.

Orange-slice Earrings

you will need

polymer clay: pearl, pale orange and dark orange

rolling pin

craft (utility) knife

self-healing cutting mat

bamboo skewer

cheese grater

2 eye pins

round-nosed (snub-nosed) pliers

2 large rings

2 earring hooks

1 Roll a 5mm/¼in diameter sausage of pearl clay. Roll the pale orange clay into a short 1.5cm/⅝in diameter sausage and cut it lengthwise into four triangular segments.

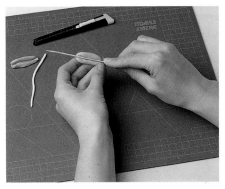

2 Cut lengthwise into two of the triangles and insert a skewer. Press the clay together to form a tunnel. Fill the tunnel with the sausage of pearl clay and reform the triangular shape.

3 Roll out a piece of dark orange clay thinly and cut strips 1cm/½in wide to fit between the segments. Arrange the pieces together to make a half cylinder. Roll out a 3mm/⅛in layer of pearl and a 2mm/¹⁄₁₂in layer of dark orange for the peel and mould these around the curved side of the cylinder.

4 Make two 1cm/½in balls in dark orange and roll on a cheese grater to make them look like small oranges. Fit an eye pin through the centre of each. Trim any overlapping edges from the half cylinder and roll the peel on a grater.

▲ **5** Cut two 5mm/¼in slices from the cylinder and make a hole in each for a ring. Bake the pieces following the clay manufacturer's instructions. To assemble each earring: using round-nosed pliers, loop the wire extending from the eye pin in each small orange and snip off any excess. Put a large ring through the orange slice and attach to the loop below the small orange. Attach the earring hook to the loop above the small orange.

Glow-in-the-dark polymer clay covered with silver leaf is embossed with spiral patterns to create an intriguing effect on this hair slide (barrette). In the dark, a subtle glow emanates from tiny cracks in the silver leaf.

Abstract Hair Clasp

you will need

½ block glow-in-the-dark
polymer clay

rolling pin

pencil, thin card (stock) and
scissors (for template)

craft (utility) knife

silver leaf

brayer

old jewellery or buttons

dark blue bronze powder

artist's brush

hair slide (barrette) clip

varnish

epoxy resin glue

1 Roll out some polymer clay to a thickness of 3mm/⅛in. Draw the shape required on card, and cut this template out. Place the card on the clay and cut round it with a craft knife.

2 Apply silver leaf to the clay shape. Roll over the backing sheet with a brayer until the leaf has adhered, then gently peel off the backing.

3 Create a regular pattern around the edge of the silvered clay by pressing interestingly shaped jewellery or buttons into it to leave indentations.

4 Fill in the central area with a random pattern applied in the same way as in step 3 but using different shapes if you wish.

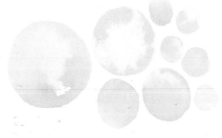

5 Lightly brush the surface around the edge with dark blue bronze powder.

◀ **6** Slip a small piece of thin card through the full width of the hair slide clip then place the clay shape on top. The clay will mould itself to the curved shape of the slide but the card will prevent it sagging too much. Bake in this position, following the clay manufacturer's instructions. When cool, varnish the surface and glue the clip on to the back.

Polymer clay simplifies the craft of jewellery-making because stones can simply be pushed into the clay. Metal leaf and powders readily adhere to the surface of unbaked clay to give it a lustrous richness.

Burnished Bronze Necklace

you will need

1 block black polymer clay

rolling pin

craft (utility) knife

bronze powders: various colours

artist's brush

leaf pastry cutter

modelling tool

jewellery wire

wire cutters

glass cabochon stones

varnish

round-nosed (snub-nosed) pliers

glass beads

necklace clasp

1 Roll out a piece of black clay, about 4mm/³⁄₁₆in thick, and cut in half. Dust lines of bronze powders in various colours on to the surface of one piece.

2 Now carefully mark vertical lines between the colours and then cut out leaf shapes in such a way that your vertical lines form the leaf's central veins. Create the smaller veins on the leaves by using a modelling tool.

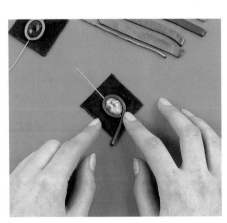

3 Roll the remaining clay slightly thinner and cut it into five or six 5cm/2in squares. Place a length of jewellery wire centrally on each square and place a cabuchon stone over it. Cut strips 3mm/⅛in wide from the remaining bronzed clay and wrap these round each stone, cutting off the excess.

4 Arrange three leaves to one side of the stone. The wire should consistently project from the same side of the middle leaf on each square, to allow the necklace to hang in a tight-fitting curve when assembled.

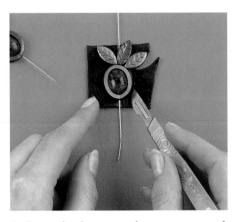

5 Press the leaves and stone surround gently but firmly enough to meld them together and to hold the stone securely in place. Cut out the black clay around the shape using a craft knife and smooth along the joins at the sides to obliterate them. Bake following the manufacturer's instructions.

6 Carefully varnish the bronzed areas and allow to dry. Using round-nosed pliers, make loops in the wire ends and trim off the excess wire. Hook the pieces together and close up the hooks. Attach glass beads at each end of the necklace in the same way to achieve the correct length. Finally, wire on a clasp.

It's hard to believe that this exotic-looking piece of jewellery is made from a piece of plastic pipe covered in polymer clay. Gold leaf and embedded stones help to effect a magical transformation.

Egyptian Bangle

you will need

4cm/1½in length of plastic drainpipe

1 block black polymer clay

rolling pin

Dutch gold leaf

brayer

craft (utility) knife and ruler

self-healing cutting mat

smoothing tool

modelling tool

gemstones

epoxy resin glue

acrylic craft paints

fine artist's brush

gloss acrylic varnish

1 Roll out a strip of clay large enough to cover the section of plastic pipe. Apply the gold leaf and crackle the surface using a brayer (see Polymer Clay Techniques).

2 Cut the clay exactly to size and wrap it carefully round the pipe, making sure there are no air bubbles.

3 Join the clay, taking care not to rub off any gold leaf when smoothing over the seam where the ends meet.

4 Using a modelling tool, mark a faint line around the circumference 1cm/½in from one edge. Measure the circumference, divide the figure by the number of stones you wish to use and mark their positions along the line. Press the stones into the clay.

5 Draw a line round each stone then impress an arch around it.

6 Draw a line around the bangle joining the tops of the arches.

7 Etch a narrow petal shape between the arches all round the bangle to form the centre of the stylized flower.

8 Draw a pointed petal on either side of the central one then add smaller petals in between.

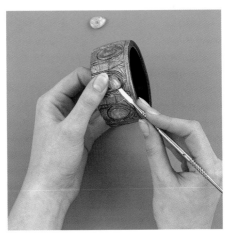

9 Carefully remove the stones and bake the bangle following the clay manufacturer's instructions. When cool, glue the stones back in place.

10 Paint the flowers and background sections in colours of your choice. Finish with several coats of gloss varnish to protect the paint and gilding.

The tiers of these glamorous but lightweight earrings swing when you move and glitter as they catch the light. Gold leaf scrolls, gemstones and droplet beads all contribute to the opulent effect.

Shimmering Earrings

you will need

jewellery wire

ruler

wire cutters

round-nosed (snub-nosed) pliers

½ block black polymer clay

rolling pin

craft (utility) knife

Dutch gold leaf

brayer

gemstones: oval 1cm/½in long;

rectangular 1.5cm/⅝in long;

round 5mm/¼in diameter

dressmaker's pins

palette knife (metal spatula)

eyelet or similarly shaped object

smoothing tool

gloss acrylic varnish

paintbrush

large clip-on earring backs

epoxy resin glue

10 droplet beads

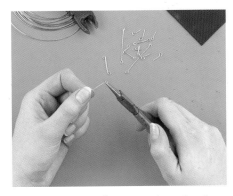

1 Cut 12 x 2cm/¾in wire lengths; form a loop in one end of each. Cut two 3cm/1¼in lengths and two 6cm/2½in; loop all ends. Roll out the clay, cut in two and gild one half. Cut backing sheets from ungilded clay: two 3cm/1¼in squares (for the top tiers); two 4 x 3cm/1½ x 1¼in oblongs (central tiers); two 1.5cm/⅝in squares (bottom tiers).

2 Lay three short wires along the bottom of each middle-sized backing sheet and press them in with the brayer. Lay a long wire down the centre of each large backing sheet with a short, single-hooked wire on either side, and press in. Lay the remaining short, single-looped wires one on each of the small backing sheets and press in.

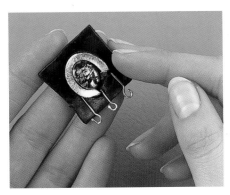

3 Press an oval stone on to each of the middle-sized backing sheets. Cut two strips 3mm/⅛in wide from the gilded clay and wrap securely round each stone, trimming off any excess. Add more strips to decorate.

4 Cut two 3cm/1¼in lengths of gilded clay. Pinch both ends to taper, shape into scrolls and press on to the mid-sized backing sheets to cover the wires. Cut two small squares of gilded clay, cut in half diagonally and place above the scrolls. Press decorative marks and lines around the border with a pin. Trim off the excess backing sheet. ▶

5 Press the square stones centrally on the two large backing sheets. Cut a 1.5cm/⅝in square and a 1cm/½in square from gilded clay, then cut across to make four triangles. Press a large triangle above each stone and a small one beneath. Cut four thin strips of gilded clay to fit on each side of the stones.

6 Using a palette knife, press in all the pieces to make a tight fit round the stones (avoid distorting the shapes). Cut two thin strips 4.5cm/1¾in long from the gilded clay, curl them into scrolls and place one under each bottom triangle. Use an eyelet to stamp a circular design on the top triangles.

7 Make six tiny beads, roll them in gold leaf and use them to decorate the tops of the middle tiers. Trim off the excess backing sheet.

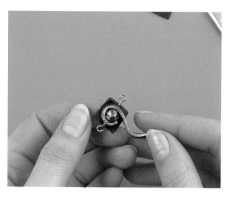

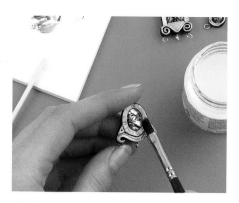

8 Place one of the remaining stones on each of the small backing squares. Cut two strips of gilded clay 3cm/1¼in long and wrap them round the stones. Trim off the excess backing sheet.

9 Using a smoothing tool or your finger go round the edges of each piece to make sure all the surfaces are melded together. Bake following the manufacturer's instructions and allow to cool.

10 Varnish all the gold leaf surfaces and allow to dry. Glue the clip-on earring backs to the backs of the first tier.

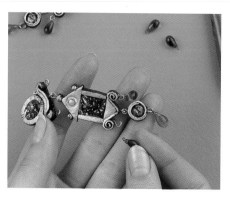

11 Join all the tiers of the earrings together, using round-nosed pliers to close up the wire hooks.

12 Hang droplet beads from the free hooks, closing up the hooks. The droplets at the bottom can be slightly bigger than the others.

You can use the art of making clay canes (see Polymer Clay Techniques) in many exciting ways. Here, in a technique known as millefiori, slices from different canes are applied to partially baked polymer clay beads.

Composite Beads

you will need

1 block white polymer clay

rolling pin

craft (utility) knife

tissue blade

¼ block yellow polymer clay

1 block green polymer clay

Perspex (Plexiglas)

½ block fluorescent orange polymer clay

¼ block pale blue polymer clay

6cm/2½in of 3cm/1in diameter picture cane (see Polymer Clay Techniques)

20cm/8in flower cane

½ block coral polymer clay

polymer clay beads in various shapes (see Polymer Clay Techniques)

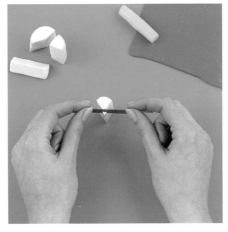

1 Roll a 3cm/1¼in diameter log of white clay. Cut it into five wedges from the centre and slice off the sharp angle of each wedge. Roll out a 6cm/2½in yellow cane and a flat sheet of green clay.

2 Arrange the white triangular wedges, separated by 3mm/⅛in slivers of green, around the central yellow cane to form a flower. Roll, using a sheet of Plexiglass to smooth.

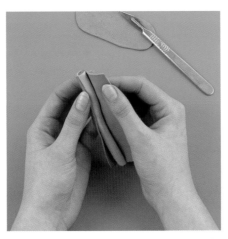

3 Make a jelly roll with 4 x 10cm/1½ x 4in strips of yellow and fluorescent orange clay (see Polymer Clay Techniques). Wrap it in a sheet of pale blue clay about 1mm/¹⁄₁₆in thick.

4 Reduce the picture cane to a diameter of 1cm/½in and the flower cane and jelly roll to about 5mm/¼in (see Polymer Clay Techniques). Reserve the trimmings to make beads. Cut the jelly roll into 7.5cm/3in lengths. Cut a 7.5cm/3in length from the duck cane. ▶

5 Cut the flower cane into four lengths of 7.5cm/3in. Arrange them in a cross pattern around the picture cane, interspersed with four lengths of jelly roll cane.

6 Roll the assembled canes carefully between your hands to meld them together then wrap in a 3mm/⅛in thick sheet of green clay.

7 Cut the cane in half using a tissue blade, rocking while you cut to avoid distorting the picture. Wrap one of the halves in a 3mm/⅛in thick sheet of coral clay, cut off the surplus and roll under Plexiglass to smooth the sides.

8 Make up several compilation canes then reduce them further to different sizes. Shave off thin slices to cover the surface of previously prepared disc beads and roll them smooth. It is a good idea to make the canes and the beads compatible sizes.

9 Use some of the surplus picture and flower cane to make borders or sides for the beads. Press them on firmly so they will adhere, then smooth over.

10 Cover previously prepared round beads, filling any triangular shaped gaps with slices of the surplus small flower or picture cane. If you cover any bead holes, pierce through again after you have rolled the surface smooth. Bake all the beads following the clay manufacturer's instructions.

This delicate little glass box is ideal for storing small pieces of jewellery such as earrings, and makes a pretty ornament. Opal glass, available from stained glass specialists, adds an extra-special lustre.

Opal Glass Box

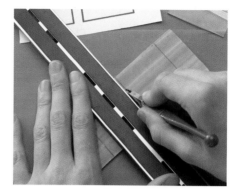

1 Trace the templates provided for this project at the back of the book, enlarging to the size required. Transfer the shapes to the glass using carbon paper. Using a cutting square or a thick straight-edge, score and break the side pieces of the box from clear glass and blue glass. Transfer the octagonal base outline on to the mirrored blue glass. Score and break the glass. Smooth all the edges with a scythe stone dampened with a little water.

2 Wrap the blue side pieces in 6mm/¹⁄₄in copper foil and the thinner clear picture glass in 4mm/³⁄₁₆in foil. Press the foil down firmly using a fid.

3 Apply 4mm/³⁄₁₆in copper foil around the top surface of the mirror base to ensure that the sides bond securely. Wrap the sides using 6mm/¹⁄₄in copper foil. Press down firmly with a fid.

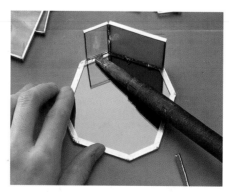

4 Brush all the copper-wrapped pieces with flux and lightly tack-solder the side pieces into place around the base of the box, adjusting them slightly to fit together if necessary.

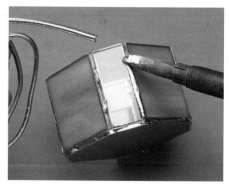

5 Reflux and solder all copper surfaces. For a neat finish, run a bead of solder to fill the point where the side sections meet. Wash thoroughly to remove any traces of flux.

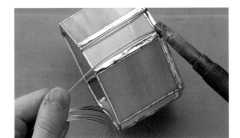

6 With the box balanced on one side, hold the end of a piece of wire just overlapping one of the clear glass sections. Brush with flux and touch the tip of the iron to the wire to solder it. Trim off the other end with wire cutters and repeat, applying two vertical wires over the clear glass panel.

7 Solder two horizontal pieces of wire to the pair of verticals. Solder them on oversize, then trim them to length when they are soldered in place. Wash thoroughly to remove any traces of flux. Repeat steps 6 and 7 to decorate the other clear glass panes.

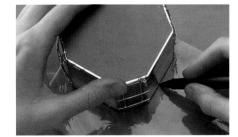

8 Lay the glass for the lid face down and place the box upside down over it. Trace around the box with an indelible black pen. Score and break the glass just inside the lines. Smooth with a scythe stone and wrap the edges of the lid with 6mm/¼in foil. Apply flux and plate the foil with solder.

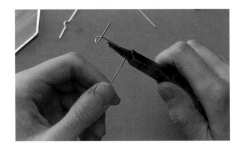

9 Cut two pieces of wire about 10cm/4in long. Using the template as a guide, bend two kinks in one piece using a pair of round-nosed pliers. Bend two right angles in the other piece of wire to coincide with the kinks in the first. Bend the two ends into loops and trim off the excess wire with wire cutters.

10 Apply flux to both pieces of wire. Solder the kinked section to the box and the looped section to the lid. Wash thoroughly to remove any traces of flux. Slot the lid hinge section into the body section to complete the box.

Patterns for some of the projects are given here so you can make templates. The way you copy these may depend on the materials being used, but cutting out a card template and drawing round it is often the best approach.

Templates

Tracing

Unless you have access to a photocopier, you will need to trace the printed pattern before transferring it to a piece of card for cutting out.

1 Use a pen or pencil to draw over the image. Turn the tracing over on a piece of scrap paper and use a soft pencil to rub over the lines.

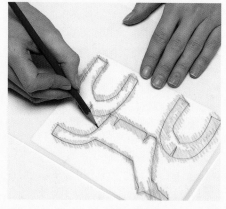

2 Place the tracing, right side up, on a sheet of paper or card (stock). Using a hard pencil, draw firmly over all the lines of the design.

3 Lift off the tracing to reveal the design. Go over the lines if necessary before cutting out the template.

4 When working with fabric, it may be possible to trace the design directly using a fabric pen. Tape the drawing to a light box or window and tape the fabric over it to hold it still while you draw.

Scaling up

You may want to make a template that is larger than the printed design. Scaling up is easily done using a photocopier with an enlarging facility, but failing this you can use graph paper. For very small designs, scaling down may be required.

1 Trace the design and tape the tracing over a sheet of graph paper. Using an appropriate scale, draw the design on a second piece of graph paper, copying the shape from each small square to each larger square.

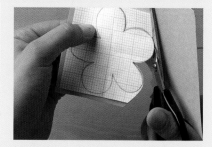

2 Lay or paste the graph paper template on a sheet of card and cut around the outline.

Enamelling and Metalwork Templates

Bird Lapel Pin, p20

Fishy Cufflinks, p34

Banded Ring, p32

Two alternative designs are shown here

Stargazer Earrings, p36

Pet Brooch, p38

Flower Pendant, p40

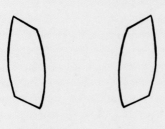

Shield Earrings, p42

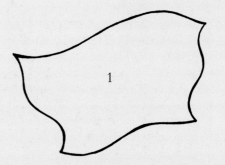

Wave Brooch, p45

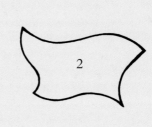

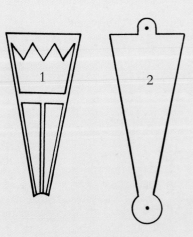

Triangular Pendant, p53

Cloisonné Earrings, p48

Paper, Card and Wood Templates

Fruity Bracelet, p72

Sun and Moon
Badges, p81

Winged Cupid Brooch, p76

Shooting Star Badge, p84

Crab Jewel Box, p86

Clay and Glass Templates

Moulded Star Earrings, p100

Florentine Boxes,
p104

Opal Glass Box, p120

Lid and base

Side pieces

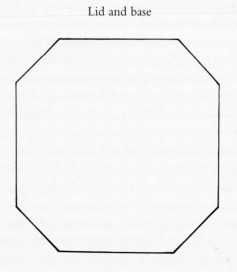

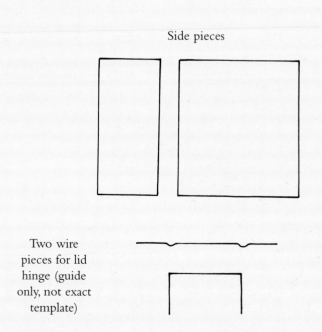

Two wire
pieces for lid
hinge (guide
only, not exact
template)

Index

Acknowledgements

The publishers would like to thank the following people:

CRAFTSPEOPLE

Ofer Acoo: Spider's Web Brooch p60, Moulded Star Earrings p100, Sun and Moon Earrings p103. **Marion Elliot:** Painted Tin Brooches p58, Rolled-paper Beads p74. **Sophie Embleton:** Fruity Bracelet p72. **Lucinda Ganderton:** Florentine Boxes p104. **Dawn Giullas:** Pocket Clips p56. **Jill Hancock:** Sun and Moon Badges p81, Sunflower Badge p82, Shooting Star Badge p84. **Kitchen Table Studios:** Egyptian Bangle p112. **Mary**

Maguire: Furry Flower Necklace p57, Spider Buttons p102, Abstract Hair Clasp p108, Burnished Bronze Necklace p110, Shimmering Earrings p114, Composite Beads p117. **Jane Moore:** Banded Ring p32, Fishy Cufflinks p34, Stargazer Earrings p36, Pet Brooch p38, Flower Pendant p40. **Deirdre O'Malley:** Opal Glass Box p120. **Denise Palmer:** Plique-à-jour Earrings p30. **Maggie Pryce:** Decoupage Roses Box p78. **Kim Rowley:** Star-sign Brooch p71, Winged Cupid Brooch p76. **Ruth Rushby:** Bird Lapel Pin p20, Gold Foil Beads p22, Cloisonné Earrings p48, Cloisonné Brooch p50, Triangular

Pendant p53. **Sarah Wilson:** Reptilian Ring p24, Striped Necklace p27, Shield Earrings p42, Wave Brooch p45. **Dorothy Wood:** Orange-slice Earrings p107.

PHOTOGRAPHY

Karl Adamson, Lisa Brown, Steve Dalton, Nicki Dowey, James Duncan, John Freeman, Michelle Garrett, Janine Hosegood, Tim Imrie, Gloria Nicol, Lizzie Orme, David Parmiter, Debbie Patterson, Debi Treloar, Peter Williams.

Thanks also to the authors, stylists and illustrators whose work is featured in this book.